Our Disunited States of America:
The Struggle Between Conservatives and Liberals

By Donald Jansiewicz

© Copyright 2020 Donald Jansiewicz
All rights reserved.

No portion of this book may be reproduced in whole or in part, by any means whatsoever, except for passages excerpted for the purposes of review, without the prior written permission of the publisher.

For information, or to order additional copies, please contact:

Beacon Publishing Group
P.O. Box 41573 Charleston, S.C. 29423
800.817.8480| beaconpublishinggroup.com

Publisher's catalog available by request.

ISBN-13: 978-1-949472-05-9

ISBN-10: 1-949472-05-9

Published in 2020. Printed in the USA.

First Edition. New York, NY 10001

This book is dedicated to those Americans born between the late 1960s and the present. These younger generations are inheriting a political system that is nearly paralyzed. There is no real movement forward. The new generations certainly face some monumental challenges; but I do believe that they can repair nearly a half century of damage.

Generations X, Y and Z can fix things through policy solutions that work for most of us, not just some of us. They will do it by focusing on the real-world problems that won't go away rather than "pie-in-the-sky" doctrines.

Our Disunited States of America

1. Introduction..........................1

   THE PROBLEM
2. A Divided America.....................8
   - Two Visions of America
   - Flash Points
   - Mood Swings
3. The Disappearance of the Center..........23
   - The Old Model of Appealing to the Center
   - The New Model of Appealing to the Base
4. Our Two Fractured Tribes..................37
   - Diverse Conservative Policy
   - Diverse Liberal Policy
5. Painful Histories.........................45
   - Struggling Small Businesses
   - Forgotten Farmers/Industrial/Service Workers
   - Slavery and Segregation
   - White Fright
   - The Impoverished
   - New Immigrants
   - Disabled Outsiders
   - Painful Histories and Our Divided Nation

THE CAUSES
6. Underlying Causes............................85
    Internal
    The Social Context
    Life Changing Experiences
    External
7. Media Echo Chambers.......................104
    The Death of the Fairness Doctrine
    24-Hour Media
    Echo Chambers
8. Manipulating Outcomes.....................110
    Spreading False Information
    Gerrymandering
    Legislation and Executive Orders
    Electoral College Roulette
    Judicial Involvement

THE SOLUTIONS
9. My Way or the Highway....................122
    If Conservatives Rule
    If Liberals Rule
10. Internal Realignment........................142
    States' Rights/Interstate Compacts
    Unicameral Legislature
    Presidential Election by Congress
    Fixed Judicial Terms
11. Moderating Factors..........................147
    Population Shifts
    A Greater Role for Women
    Generational Differences

Revitalizing Rural/Small Town America
Moderation Advocates

12. Final Thoughts.................................169

APPENDIX
13. Amicable Divorce............................173
Acknowledgements
Endnotes

Donald Jansiewicz

INTRODUCTION

Vladimir Putin is smiling. He is smiling because Americans are playing right into his hands as they fight each other over a range of issues. Putin's undercover agents quietly do their work of feeding us disinformation to fan the flames. And as they do this, our political system becomes more dysfunctional and he achieves his goal of *Making Russia Great Again*.

Not a day goes by without experiencing conflicts between our liberals and conservatives. It might be at an uncomfortable holiday dinner in which somebody says the "wrong" thing. Or, it could be the two neighbors that come after each other because one of them put up a political sign that the other found offensive. Maybe it is the threatening phone call that someone receives after stating their views on some issue.

The conflict might be in such a situation where somebody gets stigmatized on campus or at work because of their political beliefs. It might be similar to California, where some counties want to split off and form a new 51st state. It could be some talk show host who gets killed for his controversial views. Just recall that shooter who had attacked

Our Disunited States of America

Republican members of Congress at their baseball game or those pipe bombs that were sent to Democrats and the media. We have a new example every day.

The time to start compromising is long overdue. As much as we might want to avoid self-destructive conflict, a potential nightmare is now in the beginning stage.

This nightmare is not to be found in the halls of Congress or in the White House. Rather, it is among the ordinary Americans who are now increasingly conflicted about the future, and other citizens who are worried about the level of conflict

Prior to the 2016 Presidential election, purchases of guns jumped up dramatically among political conservatives who then feared that the liberal candidate, Hillary Clinton, would clamp down on gun buying if she became President. They just wanted to protect themselves from any left-wing government that would be out-of-control and start taking away their Second Amendment rights.

Then, after the 2016 Presidential election, the gun purchases went up again. Only this time, those gun buyers were on the liberal end of the political spectrum. Liberal gun buyers wanted to protect themselves against the new right-wing government that they feared would go after liberals, as well as vulnerable people.

Donald Jansiewicz

Since that time, the government regulation of gun purchases has not increased, even though there has been an increase in gun violence in a number of states. Despite the protests against this gun violence, there has been no concrete action by the national government. All that really happens is a perpetual debate. It goes on and on throughout the 24-hour news cycle. The debates occur every day and tensions escalate.

As these tensions rise between these two tribes, we could descend into bitter conflict. The two sides just keep preparing for the worst and the divisions get even deeper. The echo chamber grows larger and louder. And, it is a possibility that the leadership of each tribe could be taken over by the more extreme elements.

As candidates struggle to please the extremists, both the liberal and conservative tribes could become even more polarized, as well as more unwilling to tolerate loss. If there is some type of *spark* the whole thing could blow up into armed struggle of neighbor against neighbor. Just imagine the outcome!

This book has been evolving over years. I look back and think of my process of becoming a voter, and then eventually someone who analyzes politics. Although I was born during the Roosevelt administration, my first political memory (in 1952) was that of the new President, Dwight Eisenhower, the former World War II general. I was about nine years old at that time.

My parents did not talk very much about politics; my factory worker father and my 1950s housewife mother were very interested in having the government do things that would help improve our young family's future. When I got to the age of seventeen in 1960, my interest in politics was forming and I still recall the televised debates between Richard Nixon and John Kennedy.

By the time I got into my second year of college, I had made the decision to major in Political Science. I was so interested in this field that I eventually decided to teach Political Science and write about the subject. That interest in politics has continued.

From the beginning, I have seen much of American politics as a daily struggle between the liberals and the conservatives over a variety of issues, ranging from economic and social to our relationships with other countries. I am deeply concerned about this high level of conflict between these two ideological foes. It just keeps growing and growing. In fact, it is like a high-intensity reality television show, but nastier.

Our nation's future is at stake. We have no clear idea of what kind of country our grandchildren will inherit from us. Without any resolution and no clear sense of direction, the American people are turned into mere pawns and are being manipulated. Unless we have a new sense of direction, America could be so enmeshed in these internal struggles that we gradually slump into a *has been* political status, like Ancient Rome or the European empires during the 17th and 18th centuries.

In the pages that follow, I will be looking at three different topics. First, I will examine the *problem* of our excessive level of controversy and the implications for various categories of people. Then, I will turn to those underlying *causes* that are behind this problem, without ramming premature or quick fixes down your throat. Finally, I will look at a range of possible *solutions*. I have also added an appendix with one more possibility.

Both sides involved in this national divide will surely recognize some or all of the problems that exist. However, there is a tendency to move directly from the problem to the solution.

Our Disunited States of America

Such leaps in thinking ignore the reality that these problems have causes and that any meaningful solutions really need to address these underlying causes. This reality will be very hard for some to accept. The current ruling generation will most likely not take on this task. We're too busy pointing fingers at each other. It will be up to the next generations.

The political inclinations of Gen X and Gen Y are still evolving. Generation X (1961-1981) is getting settled and they are building their futures. Generation Y, known as Millennials (1982-1999), is still on the way up. They are now heading towards middle age and are attempting to cope with an increasingly unpredictable environment. Finally, there is the college and high school age Generation Z.

Generation X leans towards the left while those in Generation Y are somewhat more conservative; however, generation Y is more accepting of social differences than those born before the mid-1960s. But neither X or Y is in power at this point.

Generation X will take control and be making the decisions within the next decade, while Generation Y will get a turn in just about 20 years. After that, Generation Z will take over.

Donald Jansiewicz

Just what will generations X, Y and Z do? That is a question that they will have to answer. But, first let us look at the world that they will inherit from their elders. It is not a pretty picture. In fact, it is rather ugly.

So, let's move on and examine the major ongoing struggles that we are now facing and what is causing the struggles, as well as the range of possible solutions. The toughest job for any reader will be to *look at the evidence before jumping to any conclusion.* So, take a deep breath and begin your journey into these competing ideological visions that are now defining American politics.

A DIVIDED AMERICA

Two Visions of America

Our nation is moving down two divergent paths that have little in the way of common ground. Today, there are two large groups of ideological advocates and voters that have very strong views and are unwilling to really listen to the other side.

On the one side, there are those dedicated political conservatives who are trying to (1) maintain our country's long-standing social and economic system that emphasizes reward-for-achievement, (2) maintain stable social roles for individuals and groups, and (3) advance our nation's basic economic, military, as well as other interests within world politics.

On the other side are those ideal-type liberals who believe that our whole system needs to be reformed in order to (1) provide a much greater emphasis on equality of opportunity and results, (2) have much more emphasis on tolerance, and (3) make a better effort to work cooperatively with other nations.

Conservatives and liberals also have very divergent views on many other matters, such as climate change, guns and abortion. All of these issues can have a great impact on our lives.

On an individual basis, these American conservatives and liberals can tailor-make their views on issues. One can be quite conservative on economic matters and much more liberal on the Constitutional issues, such as the *Second Amendment*. Or, one can be rather liberal on social issues, but then quite conservative on international relations or foreign policy.

On the whole, though, there are two broad visions for America. One is the conservative vision and the other is the liberal vision. Where can we find them?

According to a 2017 Gallup Poll, the ten most conservative and liberal places to live in the United States[1] are as follows:

Most Conservative	Most Liberal
Wyoming	Vermont
North Dakota	Massachusetts
Mississippi	Connecticut
Oklahoma	New York
Alabama	Washington
Arkansas	Maine
Idaho	California
Louisiana	Oregon
Montana	Maryland
Utah	Hawaii

Our Disunited States of America

Conservatives and liberals are not simply limited to these states. They can be found in all types of jurisdictions (cities, counties, towns or villages) and struggles between them are not only defined by the geographical boundaries. There are also diverse views within a state or within one of its communities.

In fact, it is not at all unusual for neighbors to have very different views on politics. Moreover, there can even be different views within a family. That is why discussing politics is often avoided at holiday dinners.

In this chapter, we will examine the views of both conservatives and liberals in more detail. Then, we will look at what happens when some issues or "flash points" are raised. After that, we will focus on how the American political system has been going through "mood swings," wrenching back and forth between the two visions and never getting a permanent feeling that things are being resolved.

Donald Jansiewicz

The Conservative Agenda

Let us begin with a profile of an ideal conservative. There are four dimensions to this profile:
- Economic policy
- Constitutionally-protected freedoms
- Social policy
- International relations

In terms of *economic policy*, conservatives believe that the national government should play a minimal role in the economy and let the capitalist system function without government interference. They believe that businesses have the right to (1) use our natural resources in order to provide the products that meet our economic demands, (2) enter new markets, and (3) pay workers with rates determined by supply and demand.

In addition, these conservatives believe that those same businesses should be free to pursue their economic opportunities and that any wealth that they gain should be distributed based on natural economic forces. Those that come out on top will do so because of their skills and their efforts. Those who end up at the bottom do so because they simply lack the skills and fortitude.

Conservatives are also deeply attached to the basic freedoms that are guaranteed in the *U.S.*

Constitution's Bill of Rights. In particular, the conservatives focus on the *First Amendment* which guarantees the freedom of religion, speech, assembly and the right to petition. Moreover, many of these conservatives are also quite attached to the Constitution's *Second Amendment* that guarantees the right to keep and bear arms.

With regard to *social policy* or ways of shaping our society, conservatives are generally trying to maintain a society in which our traditional values are honored, and in which there is great emphasis on social normality. To that same end, the traditional marriage between a man and a woman is seen as the appropriate sexual relationship. Other types of sexual relationships are viewed as being both quite deviant and undermining social stability.

Moreover, the conservative social norm is that any pregnancy should always result in the birth of a child. For the conservatives, it is <u>not</u> (and never should be) a matter in which a woman has the *choice* of whether to continue or to prevent the child's birth. The unborn child's life is so much more important than the woman's preferences.

From the conservative perspective, women do play a very special role in our society as wives and mothers. However, conservatives think that women are also able to rise to positions of professional responsibility or to achieve economic or political power—if they have the ambition and skills.

In maintaining a stable society, the conservatives believe that legal immigrants need to weave themselves into the larger social fabric and not keep focusing on their separate identities. And, as far as illegal enterers, they should just be sent back to where they came from.

Conservatives also tend to have somewhat mixed feelings on the African-American population's place in our society. On one hand, conservatives feel that it was wrong to enslave black men and women during the early days of our nation. Yet, the conservative believes that there has been over one hundred and fifty years, or eight generations, for black Americans to "pull themselves up by their boot straps".

Similarly, conservatives also keep emphasizing that Latinos and other minorities should stop focusing on their differences and should instead climb the ladder so that they too can be like other Americans.

Where a conservative comes down the strongest (in terms of preserving social stability) is with regard to crime. Conservatives believe that criminal behavior should not be tolerated. The offenders should be caught and punished for their crimes. If crimes result from drug abuse, these criminals should be held responsible and serve time in prison. Then, in order to really accomplish this, our country should have enough prisons for these drug abusers as well as other serious offenders.

When it comes to *international affairs*, American conservatives take the position that the United States must pursue its national interest and maintain a position of great strength in world politics. This calls for a very strong military presence. The United States may also enter into international agreements, but our government should not remain in any of these agreements or treaties if they might compromise our nation's economic interests or America's capacity to take a major leadership role in international matters.

The Liberal Agenda

Now, let us take a good look at the profile of an ideal-type liberal. With these liberals, the picture is also quite complicated. As in the case of the conservatives, liberals can also be analyzed in four policy areas. There are the same categories for this liberal profile:

- Economic policy
- Constitutionally-protected freedoms

- Social policy
- International relations

In terms of *economic policy*, the liberals favor some government regulation of various aspects of the economy in order to assure that businesses are behaving properly and are not engaging in dishonest or dangerous practices. The liberals also favor the programs that would create a "safety net" to prevent people from falling into poverty. Also, they favor certain programs that provide educational, as well as other opportunities, for poorer individuals so that they can move up the economic ladder.

In terms of *Constitutionally-guaranteed freedoms*, liberals have mixed feelings. The *First Amendment* freedoms of speech, religion, assembly and petition are supported, except when those freedoms are used by some individuals and groups to promote hate and discord. Also, the *Second Amendment* or the "right to bear arms" is usually recognized by liberals, but liberals believe that this right is not unlimited. Liberals contend that the government has an immense responsibility to regulate those weapons that can and have often been used to murder individuals and large numbers of people.

Our Disunited States of America

When it comes down to *social policy*, liberals are inclined to accept options that would transform our social relationships. A traditional marriage between a man and a woman is seen as typical by liberals. However, liberals are also willing to recognize marriage between individuals who share the same gender. Moreover, from the liberals' perspective, those individuals who are transgender (their sexual identity does not match physical characteristics) are seen as just another variation in a complicated world. And, when it comes to the abortion issue, it is the liberal who believes in the woman's right to choose whether or not to terminate her pregnancy.

Liberals also tend to be more welcoming of new immigrants and advocate for sanctuary cities in order to create safer places for these newcomers so that they can begin their lives in their new land. When it comes to the race issue, American liberals are much more sympathetic, given those challenges faced by black Americans, and the liberals seek to find additional ways of integrating African-Americans and other minorities into the larger society.

With regard to crime, liberals are more inclined to favor government policies that seek to create more avenues where these criminals can be reintegrated into society rather than having our government keep building more prisons. Moreover, liberals are more inclined to see the drug abuser as being someone who needs help and support rather than more jail time.

In terms of *international affairs*, liberals are much more inclined to establish more positive relations with other countries and international organizations, even if these policies might have higher economic costs. Some of these higher costs are the outright expenditures to support cooperative activities. Some of these higher costs can be measured in terms of those U.S. jobs that end up moving overseas.

Putting It All Together

Let's now look at the big picture in terms of these struggles between liberals and conservatives.

The two sides go in very different directions and then keep coming after each other on these economic, constitutional, social and international issues.

There may be a new issue every day on the front burner, yet these basic differences are permanent and never really get resolved. Just think about all of the political drama that has occurred within the past year.

Our Disunited States of America

Flash Points

Here is a list of flash points or code words that are guaranteed to motivate increased levels of conflict between conservatives and liberals, increasing the divide within the nation. Think about what these words mean to you. Then, think what they might mean to those on both sides of the country's political divide.

■ Government Regulations ■ Deficit ■ Welfare ■ Fracking ■ Terrorists ■ Offshore Drilling ■ Coal Burning

■ Mass Shootings ■ Bathroom Bill ■ Race Card ■ Gay Marriage ■ Guns ■ Right to Life ■ Abortion ■ Illegal Immigrants

■ Affirmative Action ■ Sanctuary Cities ■ Black Lives Matter

■ Police Brutality ■ Drug Abusers ■ Make America Great ■ Home School ■ Global Warming ■ Fake News

These words are sure to spark a debate in which the two sides come at each other with built-up anger and then repeat their particular doctrines. Neither side will want to go behind these words and try to figure out exactly why both sides are so much more focused on speaking than on listening.

Just pay attention to the people as well as the media information around you. Count how many times these types of words come up during a day or in one week. Then, just project this out to a year and you will get the sense of how prevalent this ideological struggle is for all of us.

Additionally, each side has extreme factions that will sometimes turn to violence. Conservative extremists would be in organizations such as the *Ku Klux Klan* or the *White Nationalists*. Liberals have had their *Students for a Democratic Society* (the *Weather Underground* faction) that used violence during the late 1960s, as well as extreme animal liberation and environmental groups, alongside the rioters who have disrupted urban communities in recent years.

These extremists on each side do not reflect those general views of the conservative or the liberal ideologies. But they do represent the worst that can happen with either movement. These extremists are more than willing to take actions that mainstream conservatives and liberals would not consider appropriate options.

So, where are we going as a nation? Let's examine what has been occurring.

Mood Swings
Our country has been shuffling both back and forth between these two ideological approaches throughout our modern history. Take a look at the last 80+ years as each side took its turn at providing

their new "solutions" to our country's problems, only for America to go onto a reverse course just a few years later.

More Liberal	More Conservative
	▶ Hoover 29-33
Roosevelt/Truman 33-53 ◀	
	▶ Eisenhower 53-61
Kennedy/Johnson 61-69 ◀	
	▶ Nixon/Ford 69-77
Carter 77-81 ◀	
	▶ Reagan/Bush 81-93
Clinton 93-01 ◀	
	▶ Bush 01-09
Obama 09-17 ◀	
	▶ Trump 2017

So, which of these eleven Presidents has been the most conservative or the most liberal? One analysis[2] would rank George W. Bush as the very most conservative with Reagan as the second most conservative. The research may well need to be revisited again after President Trump's time in office is over. What about the liberal Presidents? Here, it is a tie between Jimmy Carter and Barack Obama. Both advocated for the same type of liberal agenda.

Now each time a new crowd comes into DC town, whether they are conservative or liberal, they carry their agenda along with them and bring their "new" ideas for our country.

	Conservatives	Liberals
Economic	Protect Free Market	Regulate as Needed
Constitutional	Original Meaning	Adapt to Change
Social	Traditional Values	Accept Differences
International	America First	Seek Cooperation

Each time their agenda is formulated into public policies, only to be reversed or significantly modified a few years later.

This is literally a back-and-forth government, in which the citizens cannot predict with much certainty what their lives will be like in a couple of decades or what our country will be like for the coming generations (both their children and grandchildren).

Why do we have a type of government that is characterized by such back-and-forth mood swings? Why does that happen? Those are very important questions and that will be addressed in the following chapter.

Donald Jansiewicz

THE DISAPPEARANCE OF THE CENTER

Once upon a time, our political parties tried to win and hold office by appealing to the center, those voters who were moderate in their views. They did so because that was a successful way to win office and get re-elected.

The Old Model of Appealing to The Center
In the old model, politicians appealed to the center because that is where the most voters were. The following chart illustrates this. Those with the very strongest views (liberals on the left and conservatives on the right) do not have enough voters to win. This is because these voters were in a *normal distribution* with the largest share of the voters in the center and smaller shares of voters at each end.

Our Disunited States of America

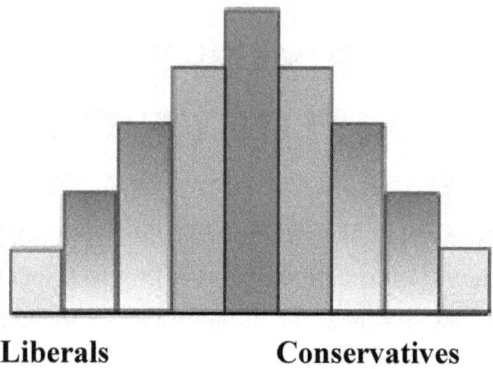

Liberals   **Conservatives**

By moderating their views in order to reach more voters, political parties and candidates were able to keep most of their ideological purists or base supporters and simultaneously pick up the additional voters from the much larger middle ground. Those political candidates who insisted upon appealing only to their ideological base were then practically guaranteed to lose the election.

A New Model of Appealing to the Base

Oh, but times change and these changes are quite dramatic! This "new normal" in American politics is our ideological or base-driven type of politics, in which purists on either side form a solid core of votes (as well as money) and are on their path to electoral victory.

Rather than the voters being distributed in a normal distribution (with most of them being in the center), they are now distributed in a *bimodal distribution* (with their voters now distributed into two groupings). One mode is on the left, the other is on the right, and not very many are in the center. In order to win elections today, it no longer makes good sense to just appeal to the center. Instead, a winning strategy now is to appeal to the political party's base.

The following chart illustrates what this bimodal distribution looks like. You will see that the mid-point is not well-populated. In fact, the high points are both to the left and to the right of the center. So, these parties and the candidates absolutely need to be extremely loyal to their base voters, alongside the hope that they can coax some from the middle to jump on board and thus win the election.

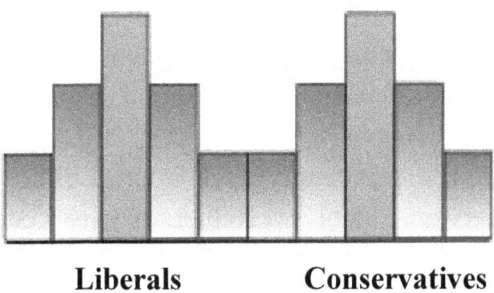

Liberals   Conservatives

Even though a substantial number of voters might regard themselves as being moderate, these ideologically-driven candidates and their ideological electoral followers have all but eliminated the moderate option. Today's party candidates are now mostly focused on their base. So, these moderate voters have virtually no choice but to switch back and forth between the conservative and liberal options.

Exactly how and why did this shift from a normal distribution to a bimodal distribution of voters occur? There are at least three reasons for this significant change.

The first reason is the *disappearance of political machines* in American life. In the old days, these political machines were the means of getting elected to office. The machine politicians normally just passed out jobs, contracts and other favors to those who were loyal to that machine's political leaders.

These machine politicians would then call the shots and design the policies that would favor their growing base. The "bosses" of the political machine did not really think in terms of liberal or conservative ideology. Rather, they just focused on getting elected and rounding up enough voters to assure this. Most machines had a local base, but could be expanded to a much larger geographical area. Coalitions of these political machines could even play a role in state as well as national politics.

Donald Jansiewicz

Then, machine politics disappeared in our system of government as our country adopted certain reforms. Today, government jobs are filled by having individuals pass civil service exams, not through political favors. In addition, government contracts for new projects are currently being awarded on the basis of competitive bids, and these same contracts are now being given to the lowest bidder. In fact, politicians would be charged with a serious crime if they distributed any type of material favor in order to "buy" voters.

In addition to the disappearance of machine politics, our system has been transformed from a normal distribution to a bimodal distribution through a much *greater role for the media* in American political life. Today's media reaches millions and millions of people each and every day through radio, television, the internet and social media outlets. The media is the modern means for "spreading the word."

Ideologically-based messages now emanate from sources that are within the two camps. These sources have a guaranteed audience and these sources simply "preach to the choir," their loyal followers. Then, the target audience responds by delivering votes, funding, and other resources to achieve the desired political goals. After that, the process of distributing the one-sided information and the response by loyal voters is repeated all over again.

This major role of the media greatly expanded when something called the *Fairness Doctrine* was eliminated in American politics.

The *Fairness Doctrine* was first introduced by the FCC (Federal Communications Commission) in 1949 and it required broadcasters to present both sides of controversial issues. Under the *Fairness Doctrine*, the broadcasters had to devote some of their airtime to the important, as well as controversial, issues—and do so in a way that was "honest, equitable and balanced."

Broadcast stations could do this through the news segments or other media approaches, such as commentary or editorials. Equal time was not required; the *Fairness Doctrine* simply required that contrasting views be presented.

The FCC eliminated the *Fairness Doctrine* in 1987, and new, ideologically-based media operations began to form. They have since altered our political landscape.

After the *Fairness Doctrine* was no longer applicable, the broadcast media was allowed to take positions on various political issues and then spread the word out to their target audience, as well as to the general population.

In addition to eliminating the *Fairness Doctrine*, the Federal Communications Commission has recently allowed media companies to now own multiple outlets in the same local marketplaces, thus reducing the number of competing points of view. Americans then began to find the same sort of messages on local television and radio stations as well as in local newspapers.

This multiple-media ownership coupled with the elimination of the *Fairness Doctrine* has now created an environment in which the media has the potential to frame messages directed at a target audience. Today it is about the messengers telling their selected listeners/viewers/readers only what they want to hear. And the possibility for biased messaging has a much greater potential as one moves from the center out to the very left-wing and the very right-wing media outlets.

The days of fair and unbiased news may well be a thing of the past. Many media operations are becoming linked to one side or the other in America's ideological struggle.

So, let's look at how today's media is distributed in terms of ideological bias. At this point in time, according to the Pew Research Center, the following media outlets[3] now focus on their liberal or conservative audiences:

Media Sources and Ideological Orientations	
Very Left Wing ■ New Yorker ■ Slate	**Very Right Wing** ■ Breitbart News ■ Rush Limbaugh ■ Sean Hannity ■ The Blaze ■ Glen Beck
Moderate Left Wing ■ Daily Show ■ The Guardian ■ Al Jazeera America ■ NPR ■ Colbert Report ■ New York Times	**Moderate Right Wing** ■ Drudge Report
Slight Left Wing ■ Yahoo News ■ Wall St. Journal ■ CBS News ■ Google News ■ Bloomberg ■ ABC News ■ USA Today ■ NBC ■ CNN ■ MSNBC ■ Buzzfeed ■ PBS ■ Huffington Post ■ Washington Post ■ The Economist ■ Politico ■ BBC	**Slight Right Wing** ■ Fox News

It is obvious that the left-leaning or liberal media sources outnumber conservative media sources. Basically, this reflects the evolution of the media industry. The larger number of liberal leaning media sources does not mean that the liberal audience size is larger than the conservative audience. These two tribes, liberals and conservatives, are both large, but the liberal media outlets have been around for a much longer time period. Media outlets like the *New York Times, Wall Street Journal, ABC, NBC* and *CBS* have been active for generations. *Fox News*, by contrast, was launched in 1986.

This liberal orientation of many established media sources helps us to understand why the conservative media sources see themselves as being the response to the liberal media. Consequently, the conservative media appeals to those who are both disaffected and alienated from liberal viewpoints. It also helps us to understand why some of the conservative politicians are quick to criticize most media sources that are not aligned with their viewpoints and then accuse the media of lying or perpetuating "fake" news.

There will be more information on liberal and conservative media later in the book. Now let us turn to the newest media sources that have evolved in recent years.

The role of media would not be complete without including social media. *Facebook, YouTube* and *Instagram* are the big players. They are followed, in overall audience size at this time, by *Twitter, Reddit, Pinterest, Vine, Ask.fm, Tumblr, Flickr, Google+, LinkedIn, VK, Classmates* and

Meetup. The messages that start from any single source, or a few sources, then multiply and reach millions of users as they expand over the social media network.

There is probably no better example of this than how Russians used social media in the 2016 Presidential election to disparage one of the candidates and influence the results. Social media spread the word from ideological purists to like-minded people.

The final reason for the ascension of this bimodal politics is the role of *Big Money* in American political life. Both individuals and organizations are free to raise and contribute money to those whose positions they favor on issues.

Restrictions on such funding are quite limited. Big Money is then able to buy political advertising, fund certain candidates, and then hire full-time lobbyists to shape public policy year around—by providing one-sided information to those political decisionmakers in the Congress and White House, as well as administrative agencies and regulatory commissions.

Big Money is also able to set the agenda and get control of our political lives by shaping the very messages that are heard and viewed by the public.

Donald Jansiewicz

In addition, Big Money sources can buy their way into the political decision-making process through campaign contributions (that are needed to win office), and thus gain direct contact with the members of Congress and the higher-ups in the Administration (the President, the Vice President and the Cabinet Department heads).

So, exactly who are these Big Money people and how are they linked to these liberal and the conservative political tribes? That is a good question.

The following table sums up some of the top twelve spenders (six months into the 2018 election cycle) in terms of source, amount and the distribution of funds[4] to liberal and conservative candidates.

Contributor	Amount	%Lib	%Con
Fahr LLC	$28,387,407	100.0	
Urline Inc	$26,139,461		100.0
Carpenters Joiners	$16,195,027	94.6	5.4
American Action Net	$15,352,470		100.0
Paloma Partners	$14,336,600	100.0	
Laborers Union	$12,026,226	92.8	7.2
Soros Fund Mngt	$10,323,632	99.8	.02
Renaissance Tech	$ 8,603,684	51.5	48.5
Amer Fed Teachers	$ 7,901,097	99.9	.01
Dem Gov Assoc	$ 7,316,862	100.0	
Repub Gov Assoc	$ 7,034,077		100.0
Koch Industries	$ 6,451,792	0.4	99.6

Our Disunited States of America

These organizations and their contributions reflect a response to the 2016 Presidential election. Those Liberal organizations, like Fahr LLC and the American Federation of Teachers were trying to change the basic composition of the Congress. Similarly, the conservative organizations like American Action Network and Koch Industries (the Koch brothers) wanted to maintain conservative control of the Congress.

However, these big money organizations are not nearly as discreet as the behind-the-scenes 501 (c) or *dark money* organizations that do not have to reveal the names of their contributors. In the same 2018 time period, the very conservative *dark money* organizations contributed $19.07 million dollars and the liberal *dark money* organizations contributed just $7.13 million dollars.[5]

So, American politics looks quite different today than in most of our history. Today's struggle comes closest to the time before the Civil War. In those years, tensions were geographically based, between the free and the slave states. Tensions between these two sides grew and grew. Then, as the plug was pulled, the North and South finally clashed.

Our nation is still recovering from that division. These Civil War loyalties are almost an add-on feature to the conflicts of today. Statues of Confederate leaders are held in such high esteem by some that religious statues seem so "minor league" by comparison.

At one time, the Democrats depended on the *Solid South* to get themselves re-elected to office. Beginning in 1939, things began to crumble when First Lady Eleanor Roosevelt became a very staunch advocate for civil rights.[6] After that, the *Works Progress Administration* or the WPA started to allocate its funds to benefit the African-American community through aid directed to black schools and hospitals.

Then, in 1941, President Roosevelt signed his nondiscrimination order for the defense industry giving African-Americans more of a role in government. Black Americans were now part of Roosevelt's *New Deal* Coalition. Some whites in the South became increasingly alienated. Then, Southern white alienation turned into open hostility when the civil rights movement took off during the 1960s, resulting in national civil rights legislation. That was the final blow.

The *Solid South* still remained quite solid. However, it switched to Republican party loyalty in order to punish the Democrats for caving to the civil rights movement. All one needs to do is to look at any one of the electoral maps that show the red states and the blue states. The South used to be among the blue states but now is among the red states.

The South has elected conservative politicians for nearly a half century and that is not likely to change in the near future. This switch was a major development in American politics and is sure to result in more heated policy debates in years to come.

Now that we see that our nation is divided into two separate groupings or tribes, we can turn to examining what goes on within each tribe in our bimodal type of politics. It is rather complicated and needs careful analysis. There are lots of players in each ideological tribe and they are often moving in different directions.

Donald Jansiewicz

OUR TWO FRACTURED TRIBES

Neither the liberals nor the conservatives are highly unified groups in American politics. In fact, each side is really a collection of multiple factions, which occasionally do coalesce in order to stand up to the other side. When these factions do join together, it is only for a short period of time. After that, it is back to normal and factions in each tribe are pulled in various directions before they once again join together.

Essentially, each tribe is trying to link together two different parts of its coalition. One part is made up of those *government officials* that are elected by voters. The other part is the *electoral base* that is made up of loyal voters who cast the votes needed to win.

These conservative and liberal tribes are "sort-of-organized" as each of these ideological bases attempts to guide its elected government decisionmakers. Each side has a number of players and these same players use their assets or resources in order to try to either influence the political decisionmakers or to influence other players.

Our Disunited States of America

Single-Issue groups, *Multi-Issue* groups and the *Political Action Committees* (that are called *PACs*) try to shape government decisions to favor their particular goals. These goals can be focused on various issues such as right-to-life or gun violence, or on the more general matters like environmental pollution, the size and allocation of the national government's budget or America's overall posture towards the rest of the world.

In addition, *Big Money Organizations* try to shape public policies by funding these *single-* and *multi-issue* groups as well as the *PACs* and one of the *National Party* organizations.

The *National Political Party*—both Republican and Democrat—for each of these tribes is also a major player. Both of these national political parties are, in a sense, trying to herd the disparate parts together, with the overall goal of winning the elections for Congressional seats, as well as the very next Presidential contest.

Then, there are the *Fringe* groups that try to have an impact and influence on political outcomes by using their very unconventional and controversial techniques (peaceful or violent actions).

One of the most important political players is the *Media,* which systematically communicates the various messages that are spread throughout the tribe, as well as the general population. This *media* is made up of either conventional print, broadcast or cable media outlets or the one-sided media operations (they preach to the choir). And, of course, there is the internet, which includes social media (*Facebook, etc.*) that spreads information even more quickly to the tribal factions.

The bottom line for many of these groups is not only to influence government policy, but also, and most importantly, to energize their electoral base for the next election. Failure to keep the electoral base together can be disastrous for many of the players as well as either of the tribes.

We'll now look at each of these tribes and the many challenges they face as they try to navigate through the complex American political process.

Diverse Conservative Policy Advocates

The conservative tribe is not focused on just one specific political issue. Conservatives, for the most part, are sub-divided into four types of issues. These four issue types are those familiar themes of (1) economic policy, (2) Constitutionally-protected freedoms, (3) social policy, and (4) international relations.

Conservatives are not only going down multiple pathways; to make things even more complex, there are several conservative groups that are also trying to take the leadership position down these issue pathways. Moreover, some of these conservative groups can also get involved in multiple-issue areas. As you will see, the conservative tribe is a very complicated entity.

On the economic policy front, various business interests and the national conservative organizations (*The Heritage Foundation, The American Enterprise Institute, Americans for Prosperity, The Mercatus Center* plus *The Competitive Enterprise Institute* as well as the national *Chamber of Commerce*) make the case for specific public policies that will favor a free market system.

They also do this to encourage businesses to keep investing and grow the economy. Their basic rationale is that the real winners in the United States will be those who are much lower down on the economic scale. The economic growth and this prosperity "trickles down" to them as the wealthier spend more and more of their money.

Donald Jansiewicz

    In terms of Constitutional issues, one of the biggest players in the conservative tribe is the *NRA* or *National Rifle Association*. The *NRA* works both day and night to get the message across that any restrictions on gun ownership are undercutting basic freedoms guaranteed by the *Second Amendment*. The *NRA* faces several challenges because gun violence happens with such frequency. But the *NRA* keeps fighting off those who would restrict them.

    Other conservative political groups, such as the *Electronic Privacy Information Center*, will certainly rise up in response to almost any possible restriction on those information channels that they are concerned about. They make their case on the *First Amendment's* "freedom of speech" clause and the Fourth Amendment's "searches and seizures" clause as well as the *Fifth Amendment's* language about self-incrimination for protecting personal freedoms.

    With regard to these social issues, one of the biggest players is the *National Right to Life* organization, which focuses on the abortion issue. There are also some groups that are concerned about sex education, as well as other groups that oppose any same sex marriage. The *American Family Association, American Vision*, the *Family Research Council, MassResistance* and *The Family Research Institute* are some of the leading

Evangelical groups that get involved in these social issues. In the area of education, the *Discovery Institute* is also a significant player for intelligent design explanations of nature, while the *Acton Institute* links religion to other issues.

On the international front, the major conservative advocates in foreign affairs are *The Heritage Foundation, The Cato Institute, The American Enterprise Institute, The Hoover Institution, The Manhattan Institute, The Lexington Institute* and *The Heartland Institute.* These are the "think tank" types of organizations that conduct research that just happens to support their own conservative views. Moreover, *The American Israel Public Affairs Committee* is also a big player when it comes to Middle Eastern issues.

Diverse Liberal Policy Advocates

Liberals also have organizations that promote their policy goals. These organizations focus on the economic, constitutional, social and international fronts. Of course, some of these groups do operate in multiple areas.

In terms of economic issues, some of the biggest liberal players are the *AFL-CIO, The Center for American Progress, The Center on Budget and Policy Priorities, The Urban Institute, The Economic Policy Institute,* in addition to *The Commonwealth Fund, AARP, The Environmental*

Defense Fund, Common Cause, Families USA and *People for the American Way.*

The most important advocates in terms of legal or Constitutional matters are the *ACLU (*the *American Civil Liberties Union), the Southern Poverty Law Center* as well as the *NAACP, Americans for Democratic Action* and the *Americans United for the Separation of Church and State.*

When it comes to the social policy issues, the following are the most important players: *MoveOn.org, Guttmacher Institute, The Open Society Foundation, The Feminist, Human Rights Campaign, NARAL (National Abortion and Reproductive Rights Action League), NOW (National Organization for Women), Planned Parenthood Federation of America, The Human Rights Campaign* and *People for the Ethical Treatment of Animals.*

Finally, the most important advocates for a liberal perspective on international matters are the *Human Rights Watch*, the *Inter-America Dialogue,* as well as *Amnesty International USA*. Other groups might get involved on an as-needed basis.

As you can see, neither the conservative tribe nor the liberal tribe is really a top-down organization. Rather, each tribe is characterized by multiple players advocating for their own specific goals. Each side, be it conservative or liberal, is being pulled both back-and-forth and in several different directions at once.

What's a Citizen to Do?

We ordinary American citizens are not quite sure of what to make of all this. The country is being moved down several different political roads at the same time. Both sides condemn the other and can't wait to get their revenge in the very next Congressional or Presidential election. This happens every two, four or six years, depending on who is up for election at that point.

Citizens keep hearing promises of better days ahead when the new tribe takes over. Inevitably, things start falling apart once again when the new agenda is put to the test and the next round of criticism begins from the other side. Then, it happens all over again and again.

But there are those who probably feel that they are outsiders, and the struggle between these conservatives and liberals does not seem to produce policy results that really help them.

Now we'll examine those specific segments of our population that might be considered outsiders. They are the ones who feel that they have been pushed aside or ignored. They are either frustrated or angry—sometimes both.

Donald Jansiewicz

PAINFUL HISTORIES

For most of us, these ideological struggles between the conservatives and the liberals are something we just think about, since we might not be on the firing line. But there are those for whom this ongoing political war has great significance. They feel the pain where others may not.

Here's a first look at those with painful histories, before we go into detail about each one.

- Small Business
- Farmers/Industrial/Retail Workers
- African-Americans
- White Nationalists & Uncomfortable Whites
- The Impoverished
- Immigrants
- The Disabled

Struggling Small Businesses

America's small businesses are often applauded as the basis of economic growth in our economy. These small businesses are the economic engines that create individual opportunities and they provide valuable services within the economy. They also create additional demands for goods and services that support their business operations. Yet today these small businesses are now facing a

Our Disunited States of America

number of challenges and many are struggling to survive.

According to the *Harvard Business Review*[7] in 2015, our country has four different types of these small businesses. They are (1) the Sole Proprietorships, (2) the Main Street kind of businesses, (3) the Suppliers and (4) the high-growth Startups. The following chart summarizes each type in terms of activity and the number of firms:

Business	**Description**	**Number**
Sole Proprietor	One Person	23,000,000
Main Street	Retail	4,000,000
Supplier	Products	1,000,000
Startup	Innovator	200,000

Small businesses are still struggling to recover from the *Great Recession* (2007-2012). Because of their limited size, small businesses are more vulnerable to any economic setbacks and it is harder for them to fully recover from a decline.

Sales for the small business sector are a critical measure of their success. Their sales fell dramatically in 2008 and have risen ever-so-slowly. On *Small Business Saturday*[8] in 2017, there was still a dip in foot traffic and overall dollars spent. This was not a very good sign. This mediocre performance in sales portends a harsh future for many small business owners.

The big businesses have been another factor that challenges the role of small businesses. These big businesses take customers away from the small businesses because bigger players are able to offer customers the same products at reduced prices. Moreover, big businesses can often persuade highly skilled employees of the small businesses to take jobs with their larger organizations.

On top of that, banks are also tightening credit for small businesses, making it more difficult for them to expand. Then, because they have not been able to expand, they are unable to bring in more customers and sales. These reduced sales then lead to an even further tightening of credit.

These businesses have also been clobbered by government policies. Policies such as higher tax rates, new health care legislation, employee safety mandates, as well as complex financial rules have made it more expensive to operate businesses and have been reducing the incentives. Small businesses are now forced to jump through hoops in order to comply with these government rules that they feel are both exorbitant and raise their costs of doing business.

Because of all these factors, small businesses are less inclined to hire new workers. When they do want to hire more labor, they find that it is more difficult to find skilled workers because the skilled labor force has slowly gravitated to larger firms.

When you add all of this together, you can see why there has been such a reduction in the number of business startups and other types of new small businesses. This is particularly true for Millennials. It appears that these Millennials are walking away from the small business opportunities and are instead building their economic futures elsewhere.

So, it is the small business owners feeling the pain. They are now fed up with all of these rules and regulations. Moreover, they desperately want the national government to stimulate the economy and reduce taxes, as well as open up more economic opportunities.

From a small business owner's point of view, national government politicians keep talking a good game, but not giving them the results.

Consequently, these owners find themselves in an unsupportive environment, and they do not know how long it will be before they have to close their doors.

Forgotten Farmers/Industrial/Service Workers

America's farmers, as well as both the factory and service workers, live in an increasingly tenuous position. What they hoped for, in their early work years, was a job that would pay good money, allow them to enjoy life, and launch their children into even better futures. From their perspective, each generation should move up a notch through an individual's hard work.

Contemporary family farmers are barely holding on, and they often need to work part-time elsewhere to provide sufficient income. They can see that many of their neighbors have given up and sold their properties to the big corporate farms. Moreover, they have also seen their own children leave and take jobs in a factory or some type of service economy organization.

Basically, the kids have "left the farm" and are now making products, working in a retail operation, or perhaps in some managerial or professional position. In any case, they are not interested in continuing the family farm. In fact, those graduating from college normally seek occupations other than farming.

Today's factory workers have joined an industrial economy that had replaced the old agricultural economy. From the very beginning of our country up through the days of Reconstruction (after the Civil War), Americans had a solidly agricultural economy. Farmers were able to make their livings and support their families by growing produce and livestock that they could take to the market.

Then, from 1870 to the 1950s, the United States was gradually transformed into an industrial economy. In the new industrial economy, the emphasis was on making things, not growing them. Children of factory workers often followed their parents into *the shop* when they were old enough. Then, by the mid-1950s, white-collar jobs surpassed blue-collar jobs.

The following chart shows the current makeup of the American economy by breaking it into three very different sectors: *Agricultural*, *Industrial* and *Service*. The numbers for each sector represent that sector's share of the nominal gross domestic product or NGDP (gross domestic product at current market prices[9] in millions of dollars). All percentages are rounded up for ease of reading.

NGDP	Agricultural	Industrial	Service
18,624,450	204,869	3,613,143	14,806,438
	1%	20%	80%

In 2016, the agricultural sector of our economy accounted for only about 1% of the NGDP. The Industrial sector accounted for a much greater share or $3,613,143.30 (again in millions of dollars). This industrial sector is eighteen times larger than the agricultural sector of the economy.

Even the agricultural sector became much more mechanized to increase output. Because of this higher productivity, American agriculture produces more than the domestic market demands. Consequently, the farmers have become much more dependent on international trade—and they have been exporting crops, such as corn and soybeans, to keep themselves afloat. Because of greater reliance on the exports, farmers are very concerned about government policies that maintain positive trading relations with other countries.

Farmers are also concerned about other public policy matters that have an impact on their employees. Because of mechanization, these farmers do not need as many employees and they don't want to pay exorbitant wages. Consequently, they end up with more illegal immigrants doing the necessary manual labor that the machines cannot perform.

Policies that are cracking down on these illegal immigrants do have a detrimental impact on the shrinking agricultural sector. Consequently, farmers are very nervous about the future, and they are now looking for somebody in Washington D.C. to look out for them. Both the liberals and conservatives seem to be looking the other way.

Even though the industrial sector is much larger than the agricultural sector of our economy, American industry is also facing multiple challenges. The future looks bleak for the typical factory worker. The industrial sector is now in decline and only represents about 20% of the nominal gross domestic product. Industrial workers want help.

Some companies are relocating their factories overseas, which reduces the overall demand for U.S. factory workers and puts great downward pressure on industrial wages and benefits. For those jobs that still remain, automation presents still another challenge, since robots can replace a factory worker and further reduce employment opportunities in the industry.

Donald Jansiewicz

Add all this to the fact that labor unions have become increasingly sidelined because they are no longer as able to negotiate wages and working conditions for many factory workers. Unions peaked when the industrial sector grew in importance within our economy. Over the years, however, the labor unions have been undermined by national and state legislation—and the union membership is in decline. Now, labor unions are increasingly remnants of the past in today's industrial economy.

Today, the industrial sector is being overwhelmed by the growth of the service sector. The children of today's factory workers are most likely to find employment in this service sector (which is now 80% of the NDGP and is four times larger than the industrial sector).

Today's farmers and factory workers now hope that their offspring will have more upward mobility and relative prosperity. This will happen for those of the younger generation who end up in a professional or a managerial position in the service economy.

However, most of these jobs in the service economy are either in the backroom supply areas or at the customer service counters. Neither of those positions pay all that well. So, the future does not look good for today's factory workers or their children.

    Because the rug is being pulled out from under them, America's industrial and service workers are angry and they are looking for answers. They continue to look towards the national government to come up with solutions that can increase their economic well-being and their long-term prospects. The conservative and liberal politicians then come up with policies that seem like band-aids that do not really increase employee opportunities. In any case, those in America's industrial sector are feeling pain.

    Just as agriculture has been downgraded (as a share of the National Gross Domestic Product) by the growth of industry, today's industrial economy has been overtaken by the new service economy.

    But does that service economy provide the higher incomes necessary to support individuals and their families? Can they build a future? It depends on whether they are *retail* or *service providers* (professionals, specialists or contractors).

    Retail employees make up only 10% of the overall workforce in the United States, and they are struggling to piece together an income that will pay their basic living expenses. In fact, sixteen million service workers make less than $15 per hour.

The following chart[10] summarizes the average hourly wages at twenty major retail companies:

Employer	Pay	Employer	Pay
Dollar General	7.87	Macy's	9.40
Dollar Tree	8.26	Walmart	9.41
Sears	8.54	Target	9.75
Ross	8.57	Bed Bath and Beyond	9.85
Kohl's	8.71	GAP	10.36
TJX	8.75	Best Buy	10.58
Toys R Us	9.00	Home Depot	11.33
J. C. Penney	9.07	Lowes	11.70
Auto Zone	9.15	Nordstrom	11.71
Staples	9.20	Costco	12.92

Most retail workers do not have the same type of benefits that have existed for other parts of the labor force. Benefits such as retirement programs and sick leave are now mostly things of the past, leaving these employees to find other ways to plan for their own future.

Many retail employees now find themselves being shifted to part-time jobs. Consequently, it is not at all unusual for the retail employees to work a couple of part-time jobs in order to earn enough money to pay the bills. Some retail employees, in fact, have large college debts to pay off, and there is no real possibility of being in the position that they imagined while in school.

It becomes even worse for the single parent who is the sole breadwinner for the family. Paying for child care is often exorbitant; even arranging for child care is a virtual nightmare if working hours keep changing and there is no backup plan to take care of the kids. They are trapped.

Slavery and Segregation
The story of black Americans is well-known, but the pain is only felt by those who have grown up with that very sad history. The very first slaves were brought to Jamestown in 1619, beginning 350 years of struggle for true freedom and justice.

The early slave trade was part of the triangular trading system. Slaves were sent from West Africa to the Americas, with some ending up in the East Coast colonies. Using this slave labor, the British colonies were able to send sugar, tobacco and cotton to Europe and trade rum and other goods for African slaves. Some six to seven million slaves were imported to the Americas this way over a stretch of time.

The role of slavery, however, substantially expanded with the invention of the cotton gin in 1793. This machine was so efficient in processing cotton that it actually increased the demand for additional slaves to bring in even more of the crop. With these slaves, plus the new cotton gin, the plantations were able to produce more cotton than they had in the previous years. Slavery became an essential asset for these plantations.

The slaves were valuable "property" at this time. Each slave that was purchased was an investment for the plantation owner and his overall profits. The owner paid about $400 ($92,000 in today's currency) per slave[11] and also paid for the slave's living accommodations, plus their food and clothing —meager as they were. Since a slave would live only about twenty years, owners wanted to make the most of their investment. The slaves were forced to work harder and longer to produce increased amounts of cotton.

Ideally, from the owner's point of view, their slaves would eventually have multiple children. The owner would then not have to pay the market value for each of the slave children, but need only provide them with food, their clothing and a place to live. In fact, the owners could—and often did—have sexual relations with the female slaves that could result in new "property" for their work force.

In order to optimize the investment of this human property, each slave had to work long hours, endure the pain of being whipped and produce a high volume of cotton or other items. What was produced, through slavery, could then be sold on the market to keep the plantations as highly profitable enterprises. Thus, the plantation owners' wealth could keep growing over the years.

Yes, there were slave rebellions from time to time and they were crushed. However, the real death knell for slavery was the abolitionist movement in the North, as well as the creation of the *Underground Railroad* that enabled slaves to flee their masters and head as far north as Canada.

Everything exploded when the Southern states rebelled and seceded from the Union. This Civil War was fought between 1861-1865, with death and destruction on both sides. Ultimately, the Northern states won the war and reunited the country through Reconstruction policies that gave new hope for the four million former slaves.

Donald Jansiewicz

When the Civil War was finally over, the new *Thirteenth, Fourteenth* and *Fifteenth* Amendments to the Constitution did in fact abolish slavery and gave former slaves citizen rights that included the ability to vote. However, the reality looked quite different than the law. Though black men and women were no longer being bought and sold, discrimination by whites continued at full force.

Southern states created laws that established what were called *Black Codes*. These laws gave certain rights to black people, but they denied them the rights to sue whites, testify against them or serve on juries. Most of the former slaves ended up as sharecroppers and paid their rent to the plantation owners by giving a portion of their crops to the owner.

Even though the Southern Blacks were "officially citizens," they were victims of white supremacists. In the late 1860s, the Ku Klux Klan (KKK) used violence to terrorize black citizens until 1871, when the U.S. Congress passed legislation that led to the arrest of KKK leaders. However, this made things only marginally better for these former slaves.

With no troops to enforce the new *Fourteenth* and *Fifteenth* Amendment rights for African-Americans, this post-war Reconstruction era came to both a very slow and painful end.

Our Disunited States of America

Throughout the South, black men and women were thrown into poverty, denied their voting rights, and faced the daily humiliation of segregation. Freed slaves were never equal to whites in the South.

Many former slaves migrated to the northern states in search of a better life. Though there were some improvements, black people were at the very bottom of the economic ladder, working in unskilled jobs with very few opportunities to move up.

Only a few African-Americans were able to find prosperity and move into professions and other occupations that paid them well. Even those who were successful faced daily barriers of prejudice from white Americans.

It was not until the federal government stepped in, once again, that opportunities for African-Americans began to slowly improve. The Supreme Court case of *Brown vs. The Board of Education* in 1954 finally opened the door for equal educational opportunities. Then, during the 1960s, in response to the civil rights movement, Congress passed the legislation that gave black citizens equal access to voting, public accommodations, education and other opportunities.

Even today, black Americans live with the feeling of being outsiders having to prove themselves before white society will take them seriously. Four hundred years have passed since the very first slaves arrived in the colony of Jamestown. Still, the burden of slavery has left its mark on African-Americans.

White Fright

All of the attention that has been focused on the painful history of black Americans has left some white Americans in a virtual state of shock about their own futures. This reaction can be called *white fright*.

There are two types of white fright. One type is that which is being experienced by *White Nationalists* and the other type is the experience of *Uncomfortable Whites*. Let me describe each.

Fundamentally, a number of *White Nationalists* contend that the United States was really founded by the white people from Europe (Spanish, British and French) and they brought the best qualities of Western European civilizations to the New World. From a *White Nationalist* perspective, those first white settlers were only able to do this because they had superior qualities of intelligence and fortitude when compared to other populations.

Essentially, *White Nationalists* contend that this has occurred through a combination of natural evolution as well as divine intervention. Over time, primitive species evolved and humans ended up at the highest level, but evolution did not stop there. From the *White Nationalist* perspective, we humans evolved into either the superior white race or into lesser humans (in the other racial categories).

For the *White Nationalists*, the final step in human evolution was the creation of the white race and those other races. God stepped in and blessed the white race with both a superior intelligence and character. Other races were not as blessed as the white race, but even they were still better off than the lower forms of life (animals).

It is true that when white Europeans came to and settled in North America, they found that other people were already in the new land. To these white newcomers, these native people were savages that needed to be controlled. White settlers did not want these primitive people to do any type of damage to their efforts to bring a higher quality of life to the new world.

Even as the years passed, white efforts to expand into the western territories had to deal with Native Americans. These indigenous tribes did not want to surrender what they still had. After several violent incidents, the colonizers generously (from the *White Nationalist* perspective) created special reservations for these primitive people. These reservations gave indigenous people a secure place to live while simultaneously keeping them from subverting white society.

Still, *White Nationalists* argue that the whites must continue to face the new challenge of other races that have tried to "invade" our country through immigration. Again, from the *White Nationalist* perspective, the inferior people have subverted the United States by trying to transform our nation by pushing whites aside.

In defense of our country, *White Nationalists* have tried to meet these perceived challenges. The nationalists believe that these groups will keep trying to get into our country and eventually try to take over. In the opinion of this group, whites intelligently restrict the number of children that they have while these inferior people keep reproducing in greater numbers.

By the middle of this century, it is predicted, those who identify as white will become a minority of the whole population in the United States. From a *White Nationalist's* perspective, whites must find some way to stop this crisis (by either closing the door, building walls or finding other ways of keeping these inferior humans out of our nation).

Our Disunited States of America

In an effort to do this, *White Nationalists* have tried to organize and take dramatic actions to put an end to these perceived threats to our national identity. From their point of view, they are doing this to preserve our nation's values and culture. Otherwise, they fear that the inferior races will pollute our culture and destroy all that is great about America. This pain is too much for the *White Nationalists* to bear.

While the *White Nationalists* feel hostility, the *Uncomfortable Whites* feel anxiety. They don't use the *N*-word or other expletives. Rather, they are very concerned about the downward evolution of our society. They don't think our government should try to prop up some groups through welfare or privileges so that outsiders get pushed to the head of the line.

As they look into the future, the *Uncomfortable Whites*' level of anxiety rises. They look at television and the world around them, and they see more and more faces that are not white. In fact, they see the other groups mingling more and more with whites. A question crosses their minds about what might their grandchildren or their great grandchildren look like. Will they be "mixed race" and will they look so different from the milieu that *Uncomfortable Whites* grew up in?

Donald Jansiewicz

Uncomfortable Whites have a history. It goes as far back as those that supported George Wallace in the 1960s and those involved in the bitter battles in New York City between black citizens and a white Board of Education during the 1960s and 1970s, as well as the busing battles of Boston in the 1970s. While some surely were overt white nationalists, many were also uncomfortable white people.

The *Uncomfortable Whites* even recall the huge feeling of shock when an African-American was elected and then re-elected to the office of President of the United States. This enabled minority populations to play a greater role in government and create new policies that handed out more benefits to those (the *Uncomfortable Whites* believed) who had not worked hard to get ahead. In an *Uncomfortable White's* mind, these outsiders basically wanted to take resources away from whites and create a complete nightmare for those who had worked for generations to build the greatest country in the world.

Uncomfortable Whites saw the 2016 election as a new opportunity to have our nation make another fresh start. The new white President would be able to cut all of the waste in government that was propping up people who did not deserve government benefits. These undeserved benefits were being paid for by hard working whites like themselves. A new President would be able "drain the swamp" and get our nation back to normal.

White Nationalists and *Uncomfortable Whites* feel pain about the world that they now live in. They look at recent changes in our political system as (1) a major way to relieve their pain and (2) a way to bring back those very qualities that enabled the United States to rise from a remote colony to the position of one of the most important nations in the world.

The Impoverished

There is yet another important segment of American population that is feeling pain—those who are now living in extreme poverty. These people often lack those basic goods and services that most of us take for granted. On average, they live on a little more than two dollars a day.

This very poor population seems to be concentrated in rural and inner-city areas. Those who are living in the suburban areas of the country are not experiencing poverty to the same degree.

According to one analysis[12] in 2018, 553 million people fall into the homeless category, an increase of 3% from the prior year. Two-thirds of these homeless are in emergency shelters and the other one-third lives on the street.

Donald Jansiewicz

Many Americans between the ages of 25 and 75 spend at least one year in poverty during their lives. During those very difficult times in their lives, these impoverished individuals have to figure out how to feed themselves and find a reliable place to spend their nights.

Poverty is not evenly distributed by age groups. The greatest amount of poverty, or 22%, is experienced by those who are age 18 and under. Nearly 17 million children in the United States are living in what can be called food-insecure households.

The situation improves somewhat for those who are between 19-21, 13.7% are impoverished. They are struggling to get launch their careers and get their lives started as independent adults.

Those who are 65 years or older are more fortunate, since only 9% of them experience poverty. That reduction in the poverty rate for seniors is primarily because Social Security and Medicare provide them with a basic income as well as medical insurance. These truly make up their safety net.

This experience of poverty in the United States also varies by racial and ethnic populations.

Our Disunited States of America

The following 2018 chart illustrates those differences:

Racial/Ethnic Category	Percent Living in Poverty
White Non-Hispanic	8.7
Asian	10.0
Hispanic	18.3
African-American	21.2

The numbers are even worse for Native Americans. In 2018, for example, 25.4% of Native Americans lived in poverty.

From as far back as 1930, the poverty numbers in America have exceeded poverty in other wealthy nations. In 2014, the United Nations expressed concern about the distribution of individual wealth and spending patterns in the United States. Moreover, in 2015, the *IMF* or *International Monetary Fund* warned America about its persistent poverty problem.

A number of factors enter in to help explain the level of poverty in the United States. One major factor is a lack of education. Another factor is the loss of one's employment while another is the family situation. In some cases, a single mother or father is the sole breadwinner for the family. This can be especially difficult when the otherwise supportive family members are spread out across the nation. A final factor in creating poverty is the racial or the ethnic category of people that limits their access to economic opportunities.

There are some other explanations, such as labeling theory (blaming the victim) and the notion of the culture of poverty (way-of-life-norms, values, behaviors of the poor) that are used to explain why poverty persists. There is also the functionalist explanation (that this poverty exists and is also maintained because these poor serve the needs of the non-poor).

One controversial explanation for poverty is based on the basic intelligence of impoverished individuals. A 1998 study by the *American Enterprise Institute* related poverty to individual intelligence quotient, or IQ, of the individual.[13] This study examined sibling pairs who were raised in the same favorable economic environment. This study found that individuals with a lower IQ earned less income than ones with a higher IQ. In the study, those with an IQ of 75 earned $11,000 whereas those with an IQ of 125 earned an income of $38,000. Based on these findings, one might conclude that the impoverished are made up of people who are not very smart.

The poverty in this country, for whatever reason, might not only lead to lower economic opportunities. Instead, it might also lead to an individual's involvement in criminal activity. There is actual evidence that supports this idea. The impoverished individual might commit a theft or sell illegal drugs, get arrested and spend several years being incarcerated. From one perspective, prisons can be viewed as warehouses for those whose life is characterized by long-term poverty.

In any case, the impoverished population in the United States faces a lingering challenge. In spite of federal programs like (1) Lyndon Johnson's *War on Poverty* and (2) recent changes in the welfare system as well as (3) the current level of employee wages and benefits, the overall situation has not really changed for millions of people. As a result, poverty has continued to be a part of our political landscape.

Instead of expanding past efforts to eliminate poverty, there has been a reversal of policy to address the poverty problem. Some people continue to make the case that recent government policies, which do away with the programs to help the poor and move towards more of a market economy, have actually had the impact of increasing, not decreasing, poverty.

The poor in America are feeling pain. This pain often finds its way into the ongoing struggle between the conservatives and liberals. Even though it is a long-term issue, there has not been any sustained effort to improve outcomes for the impoverished.

New Immigrants
America has a very complex history in terms of immigration. The new immigrants face several challenges as they try to integrate into their new country. It has never been easy—the process taking generations—and it is a difficult task for our new immigrant population.

Immigrants or refugees must find a place where they and their families can live. They need to adjust to the new culture that can seem very strange compared to where they come from. They must also learn a new language so that they can navigate their way through the complexities of American society and its economy. What's more, they must find work, so that they can pay for their family's daily expenses and unanticipated costs.

Moreover, immigrants need to find out how to get services, such as medical care or help from the government. For some, there is the real risk of deportation. Today, approximately one in four recent immigrants are undocumented. This risk of being deported is real if the person falls into the category of the *Deferred Action for Childhood Arrivals (DACA)*. These new immigrants were brought as children and can possibly be sent back to a country that they do not know.

In addition to all these other stressors, immigrants must find out how to get transportation from one location to another. Having one's own car is not often a real possibility. And of course, these new immigrants must raise their children and help them adjust to the new schools that they attend. These are not easy tasks to accomplish in an unfamiliar environment.

Imagine yourself and your family facing those challenges in a completely new country. Let us say that you were rushed into the country of Uzbekistan and had to start all over. What would you do first? What would you do after that? The challenges keep coming. How long do you think it would take before you felt comfortable?

My grandparents came to this country about a hundred years ago from Ukraine (during the post-WWI days and the unsettling times in the region). They started at the very bottom in America. Their children made it into the working class. The grandchildren, myself included, reached the middle class, but it took our family three generations. This is a very common pattern for many whose ancestors emigrated to the U.S.

    The United States has had the largest immigrant population in the entire world. Historically, immigrants have made up a little over 14% of the American population. Moreover, the United States now has about 19% of all individuals who migrated from the country of their birth to another country.

    It is now projected that the immigrants and their children could make up 88% of the population in the United States by 2065.[14] As of 2015, the following five nationalities were the very largest immigrant populations in the United States:

Source Nation	Number of Immigrants	% of Immigrants
Mexico	11,574,000	26.5
India	2,435,000	5.6
China	2,130,000	4.9
Philippines	1,942,000	4.4
El Salvador	1,387,000	3.2

Our Disunited States of America

However, these numbers do not reflect what is occurring now in terms of immigration. By 2065, Asians will be the largest group entering the United States. Recent figures indicate that the South Asian Indians are the highest at 110,000 followed by Mexicans at 109,000. This is then followed by the Chinese immigrants at 90,000. Taken together, the Asian immigrant numbers are now twice as large as the Mexican immigrant numbers.[15]

Historically, immigration into the United States has taken place in four different stages. These immigration stages are follows:

- 17th -18th centuries
- 19th century
- early-mid 20th century
- late 20th century-early 21st century

In the 17th-18th centuries immigration began with the early English settlers followed by the other Europeans. During this first period, half of these early immigrants were indentured servants. Then, in the 19th century, additional immigrants came from northern Europe. In the early to the mid-20th century, immigrants arrived from Southern and Eastern Europe. Finally, in the late 20th century through the early 21st century, immigrants came into the country from Latin America and Asia.

Donald Jansiewicz

Immigration has taken some interesting twists and turns in recent years. The *Immigration and Nationality Act of 1965* abolished an older system of national origin quotas. This then led to new immigration from the non-European countries; this has basically changed the ethnic makeup of America. European immigration dropped from 60% to 15% between 1970 and 2000. In 1990, the first President Bush increased these legal immigration numbers by 40%. Because of the changes, the doors for immigration swung wide open and our country has received millions of newcomers from non-traditional sources.

As the United States has evolved over time, earlier immigrants became much more integrated into American society and they joined the older established populations in resisting the newest immigrants, who were attempting to enter the country.

Alongside this information, consider the attack on the United States on September 11, 2001. That attack substantially increased anxiety and fear of foreigners, particularly those from the Middle East.

Resistance against new immigrants took the form of the following national government legislation or executive orders:

Our Disunited States of America

- Page Act prohibited undesirable Asians 1875
- The Chinese Exclusion Act of 1882
- The Immigration Act of 1824
- Emergency Quota Act of 1921
- The Mexican Repatriation Act 1930s
- Restrictions on Jewish Immigration early 1940s
- Operation Wetback deportation of Mexicans 1954
- Suspended entry Muslim-majority countries 2017
- Goal of 2000-mile wall U.S./Mexican border 2017
- Possible deporting of DACA

Sometimes the reaction to these new immigrants moves from a public policy response into a more violent response. This happened to Irish immigrants in the 1850s, and it happened again to Italian immigrants in 1891.

So, today's new immigrants, from the Middle East, Latin America and other areas are more than a little bit nervous. They are concerned that they could be pushed out, or that there will be other punitive actions by the United States upon their arrival. When polled, Americans feel very comfortable with the Polish, Italian or Jewish established immigrant populations, but the recent newcomers, like the Mexicans, Filipinos or other new immigrant groups, are often viewed with suspicion.

There is also a popular belief within the United States that new immigrants are more likely to engage in criminal behavior. Research on this shows that immigrants are actually much *less* likely to turn to crime. In fact, new immigrants are so fearful of deportation that they are less inclined towards crime than other populations in the United States.[16]

Another popular belief among some Americans is that these immigrants are going to take jobs away from the U.S. citizens. In fact, the new immigrants are far more likely to fill those physically difficult, low-paying jobs that Americans do not want to take.

In order to protect these immigrants from quick deportation, over five hundred jurisdictions in the United States are now actively sheltering undocumented immigrants and are not cooperating with efforts to deport these individuals. These sanctuary communities will provide food and housing, and they do not cooperate with any national government efforts to deport immigrants.

Our Disunited States of America

Efforts to do away with the *sanctuary cities* and other attempts to deport or weaken the immigrant communities give them additional uncertainty. They are now looking for the national government to help them; what they keep hearing is that their days are numbered.

Yet, surprisingly, over the last twenty-five years, according to Pew research,[17] there has been a dramatic shift in the general public's attitudes about immigrants. In 1994, 63% of Americans thought that immigrants were a large burden on American society and 31% said that they strengthen the country. Today, 59% of the Americans say that immigrants strengthened our country and only 33% say they are a burden. Quite a reversal in opinion.

Yet, within the very well-established American population (whose relatives came to the United States many years ago) there are divergent views about these immigrants. There are both important partisan, as well as generational, differences.

Our two political parties have major differences regarding the immigration issue. Those in the Republican party tend to have a get-tough stance on the undocumented immigrants as well as very strong support for building a wall between the United States and Mexico. Democrats on the other hand, have a very strong opposition to the wall, as well as a more relaxed view on how to deal with the undocumented immigrant population.

There are also significant differences between America's four generations regarding new immigrants. Compare the following generations in terms of whether they think that the immigrants strengthen America.[18]

Generation	% Agreeing
Silent Generation 1929/46	41
Boomers 1947/65	48
Generation X 1966/81	60
Millennials 1982/99	76

Being an immigrant is not easy. In fact, it is a huge challenge. Immigrants face multiple hurdles every day and they keep looking for our national government to come up with some meaningful solutions. They just keep waiting and hoping, though nothing really seems to change.

Disabled Outsiders

Americans with disabilities are also permanently sidelined in American politics. In fact, the disabled would constitute the single largest minority group (19% of our population) within the United States if disabilities were counted as a minority condition in the government's statistics.

Simply put, there are six different types of disability (hearing, vision, cognitive limits, self-care, ambulatory, and independent living). All of these types or kinds of disabilities limit the individual, and have an impact on their daily lives and their ability to play a full role in society. For them, the idea of a *level playing field* is something that they will never know.

These types of disabilities vary both in terms of the percentage of the American population that is impacted, as well as the extent that it occurs in different age groupings. A detailed summary of these six disability types[19] follows:

Disability Type	Percentage	Ages 1 - 64	Ages 65 +
Hearing	2.5	1.1	14.8
Vision	2.3	3.1	6.5
Cognitive	4.8	8.6	9.0
Self-Care	2.5	2.8	8.2
Ambulatory	6.6	6.7	22.6
Ind. Living	4.5	3.7	14.9

The individuals with **hearing** difficulty have their greatest problems connecting with the world around them because they cannot take in all the information that is being presented throughout the day. Often, they have to get their cues by guessing what other people are saying. Hearing aids are not always a practical alternative either because of the cost, inconvenience, or the fact that hearing aids generally only amplify, but do not clarify, sound.

A disability regarding *vision* can also dramatically impact an individual's life. This type of disability can range from having difficulty in seeing things to total blindness. In either case, a vision disability makes it much more difficult to take on the ordinary tasks of life. A vision disability can also have a profound effect on one's ability to take on new challenges that can build a better future.

A *cognitive disability* is an individual's limitations regarding the ability to understand and interact with the world around him or her. The cognitive limitation can be in their *intellectual functioning* (planning, comprehension as well as reasoning) or *adaptive behavior* (such as taking proper care of oneself, dressing, solving problems and following rules). In either case, those who have such a cognitive disability are quite limited as they attempt to navigate through life.

> A cognitive disability should not be confused with mental illness, which is in yet another medical category. There are millions of people worldwide that experience mental illness. In fact, one in four people experiences mental illness at some time in their lives. These mental illnesses can be anxiety disorders, mood disorders, schizophrenia, psychotic disorders, dementia, as well as various eating disorders.

Our Disunited States of America

The *self-care* disability basically means that the person cannot take care of him- or herself in regards to things that most people do normally. As a result, that individual becomes very dependent on others to help with all of the ordinary tasks (bathing, eating, using the restroom) in life.

This great dependence on others cannot contribute to an increased feeling of self-worth. There is a struggle on two different fronts: physical and emotional.

An *Ambulatory* disability can have an impact on an individual's ability to move around as others do. Some with this disability might need a cane or type of assistive device or walk abnormally, and some of those with this disability are confined to a wheelchair or something like it. Taking a swim or even walking on the beach can be quite difficult, if not impossible, for them. Shopping or traveling can also be challenging.

Finally, an inability to achieve full *independent living* is another severe disability. Because of a physical, developmental or mental condition that they have, these individuals usually have to go through their lives without being able to experience all of the aspects of the normal person's existence. Basically, they are just locked into a perpetual type of childhood and can often only attempt to find avenues for their interests. A day for them may be trying to use up their time, unless there is someone who helps them become engaged with the world around them.

Those who are disabled for any of these reasons, have much greater difficulty finding employment.[20] In 2015, about 35% of the people with disabilities were able to find work while 76% without these disabilities were able to get jobs. When they do get work, the disabled were able to earn only $21,572 per year in contrast to the $31,872 those with no disabilities earned.

The disabled are also far more likely to be plunged into poverty.[21] In 2015, 21.2% of disabled were living in an impoverished situation compared to the 13.8% of those impoverished Americans without disabilities. Furthermore, the disabled are far more likely to fall into unhealthy situations, such as smoking and obesity. It is often an uphill struggle for those with disabilities.

From the perspective of the ideological debates in this county, the disabled are not even on the agenda. Liberals and the conservatives are so busy going after each other on their "issue of the day" that they completely forget to focus on those individuals with disabilities. Their issues are simply stuck with these disabled individuals and their families. Both liberals and conservatives just walk away and focus on more dramatic matters.

Painful Histories and Our Divided Nation
There is plenty of pain to go around in American society. We have the small businesses that are struggling to survive. We have farmers, factory and service workers who face a bleak future. There are African-Americans who live day-to-day with the legacy of a history of slavery and segregation. And, we have whites who are angry or nervous about what has happened with race relations in our country. Then, we have a whole population that has been either born into poverty or has been plunged into poverty by their lives' events. After that, we have those immigrants who are anxiously trying to find their way in a new country and are not always welcomed. And finally, we also have the disabled who do not even get the sense that they count. All these people feel pain every day of their lives, and the pain does not go away. They look for help; but the help is not there.

However, this pain provides some additional fuel for those who are looking for a fight. Fighting is what these ideological tribes are really good at. We see this every day. But why is this happening? What explains the struggle between liberals and conservatives? That is our next topic

Donald Jansiewicz

UNDERLYING CAUSES

Behind every problem, there is a cause or set of causes. That is what this chapter is about. There are four different underlying causes for the ideological war that has taken over our nation. First, there is the *internal cause,* or what is going on inside the brains of those who are in the "war of words" that is now defining American political life. Next, there are those *social networks* which reinforce one's liberal or conservative beliefs. Then, there are the significant *life experiences* of those who are either on the front line, or those supporting one side or the other. Finally, there is the *external cause* of Russian efforts to change the political stage by creating conflict within the United States and European countries. Let us now examine each of these underlying causes.

Internal

Differences in human brains are a very significant underlying cause of the struggle between the conservatives and liberals. The brain is our fundamental biological base for processing information and making decisions.

You have probably heard somebody say that those on the other side (liberal or conservative) are just plain stupid. These critics are saying that the people at the other end of the political spectrum lack basic intelligence. Fundamentally, they are saying that one's political outlook is simply a matter of how smart a person is.

In fact, there is some, <u>not</u> very good[22] research, from both the liberal and the conservative perspectives that makes this case—through very sketchy, as well as very incomplete, assessments of the intelligence of those people who they are trying to deride. Those who were doing this faulty "research" did not use large enough samples or their research instruments were not very reliable. They have not repeated their studies, which is a very important part of any reliable research. In one case, there were alleged reports of research findings on political beliefs and basic intelligence from Harvard University. This research, in fact, never took place.

Even though these studies about the intelligence of the liberals and conservatives are not that useful, the brain is still an appropriate topic. It is appropriate because one can look at how the structure and the activity within the human brain shapes both the ideological beliefs and the attitudes of both liberals and conservatives.

Put simply, the brain is probably one of the most significant internal factors in shaping ideological beliefs. It is a very complex biological system that enables us to take in new information from outside ourselves, then process the information, make decisions and then respond in a variety of ways (speaking, writing, smiling, frowning, *etc.*) each day.

Our brains are the equipment with which we navigate our way through life. Without our brains, we each would just be a set of complicated physical features without a control panel. What we both think and feel is shaped by how our individual brains process the information from the world around us. This is not about our intelligence. Rather, it is about how we interact with information that comes to us.

Recent creditable research[23] has been done at *The University College in London* that focused attention on the actual brain structures of both liberals and conservatives. The research was conducted on ninety healthy young adults (roughly balanced in terms of gender) and later replicated with twenty-eight other healthy young adults. The participants ranked themselves on a five-point scale from being very liberal to being very conservative. Research subjects were then each examined with neuro-imaging equipment (Voxel-Based Morphometry and Magnetic Resonance Imaging or MRI) to determine the size and density of brain structures and relate the findings to the research subjects' self-reported ideological rankings.

This research is best thought of in terms of an ideological spectrum with strongest views at either end with many points between.

Liberals									**Conservatives**

This research focused on two very important parts of every person's brain. One part of the brain is called the *Anterior Cingulate Gyrus* and the other is called the *Right Amygdala*. These are the parts of the brain that shape ideological thinking in terms of our inclination to take in new information, as well as our emotional response to such information.

The following graphic of a human head shows, from a sideways view (facing to the right), approximately where these two very important parts of the brain are that shape one's political outlook.

Donald Jansiewicz

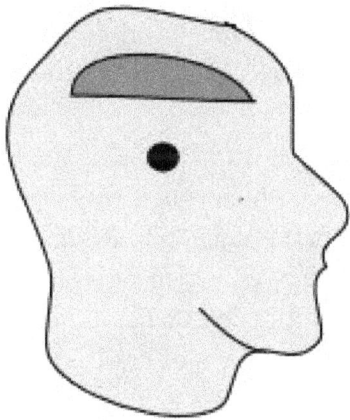

Let's now take a close look at each of these very important brain structures and see how they each have an impact on thinking about political issues.

The *Anterior Cingulate Gyrus* is at the frontal end of the **grey** area near the top of the head. It is in a curved folded area above the part of the brain (*Corpus Callosum)* which enables the communication between the left and the right brain hemispheres.

This Anterior Cingulate Gyrus is the part of our human brain that performs a number of critical functions. One of those important functions is to take in any type of new or different information, when we are making choices or decisions. In addition to taking in this new information, the

Anterior Cingulate Gyrus also tempers any fearful type of response if this information may be quite new and different.

Lower down in the same image, you will see a **black** circle, which is in a very deep part of the brain. That part is called the ***Right Amygdala***. It is the part of the brain which we use to process any emotional information that could be fearful or concerning to us. Each of us also has a *Left Amygdala*, on the other side of the brain, that can process both pleasant and unpleasant information.

According to the study, liberals generally have a larger Anterior Cingulate Gyrus in their brains due to the formation of their brain. This enables them to do much more information gathering activity. Given that this part of the brain is larger, the liberals are thus programmed to take in new and different information when making their choices. Basically, this part of the brain makes them more comfortable with the information that differs from what they are accustomed to.

Instead of having larger Anterior Cingulate Gyrus, conservatives have a larger Right Amygdala for processing the fear-based emotional information. It is larger because that is how their brains were formed. The Right Amygdala helps to process and protect an individual from anything which might be threatening. Consequently, conservatives are basically programmed to resist those things that are quite new and different—and potentially threatening.

Because of the ways their brains are programmed, the liberals are more inclined to process new and different information (and this makes the Anterior Cingulate Gyrus work overtime), while conservatives have a more expanded Right Amygdala, so they are more fearful of things that do not fit into their normal expectations. Because of these very significant differences, conservatives and liberals seem like polar opposites in terms of brain structure.

Since both conservatives and liberals are hardwired differently, these differences do show up in terms of their perception of various public policy issues. Conservatives are more fearful of change because they are programmed that way, while the liberals are more accepting of change because that is how they are programmed.

Moreover, because of these brain differences, the liberals and conservatives also seem to be differentiated in terms of their individual personalities.[24] The conservatives value stability and loyalty, and incorporate religion in the decision-making process. Liberals on the other hand, like change and new information—including sources such as scientific research.

So, it becomes more understandable why there is such a sharp divide in America on an issue such as global warming/climate change. Liberals grab onto scientific data that serves as more evidence of their claims regarding global warming, whereas conservatives doubt the scientific community and rely on scripture or other explanations.

Based on this well-tested research, we are able to predict with 71.6% accuracy who is a conservative and who is a liberal because of the differences in size of these two parts of the brain.[25] The liberals and the conservatives even have major differences in terms of how they respond to an unpleasant image. Conservatives are much more likely than liberals to look away at disgusting pictures of feces, blood or vomit.[26]

One can also predict with 69.5% accuracy what an individual's parental political views are by knowing what the individual's brain structure looks like.[27] It is quite likely that you can hold your parents partially responsible for your political views. That is, your views on issues are partially the result of genetics.

Donald Jansiewicz

Just as each one of us has inherited certain physical features from our parents and their earlier generations, we have also inherited our brain architecture (that has been shaped by those who have come before us). Certainly, each of us is an individual with distinct characteristics; each of us is also connected to earlier generations by what had been implanted through the conception process.

However, the brain is not the only factor involved in our political orientation. There are additional things which are also extremely important that shape our thinking about politics. Let us now look at them.

The Social Context

Each of us undergoes a very subtle process called political socialization which helps shape what we become. Political socialization is basically a process by which we learn about politics. This learning includes the process of building our liberal or conservative political orientations.

Basically, there are four different forces that shape our political views. These forces are the family, our peer groups, the media, and those political actors that are on the public stage and act out those dramas that are presented to us every day. The following chart illustrates how these four different political socialization forces have an impact on our political orientations.

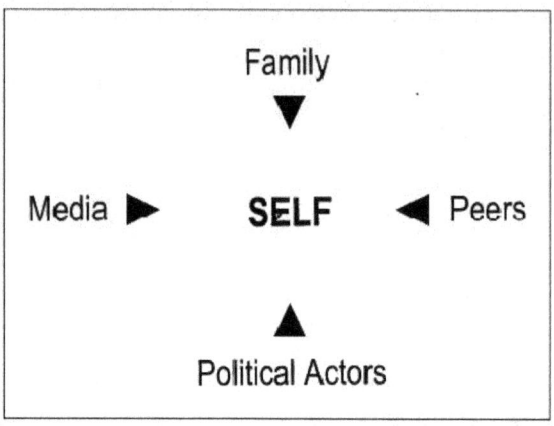

Early in our lives, our *family* (particularly parents) are the most important players in shaping our first political orientations. We all quietly observed and listened to our parents when they engaged in any discussions or activities that involved politics. Mom and Dad were our first "window on the world" of politics. They could be completely turned off and disengaged from politics, or they could be diehard liberals or conservatives. They are the ones that gave us our first messages and insights into the very mystical world of politics. Then, as a result of active and passive absorption, our political orientation is formed.

Aside from our parents, other family members can also play a role, usually reinforcing these perspectives on politics. One's brothers and sisters, as well as aunts, uncles and even our grandparents, can provide us with still more information (our early impressions), which we then use to view politics.

Also, as time passes, the *peer group* begins to serve as a virtual sounding board for one's political views. After our early encounters, we tend to associate with peer group members who tend to have a similar perspective on things political. The discussion might not be very deep or philosophical, but these peer group contacts do reinforce or somewhat modify one's belief system.

Peer groups play a bigger and bigger role over the years. Our friends in the late teen years, early twenties and into the thirties tend to impact our political orientation by either continuing the process of reinforcement or providing us with new information that challenges our previous ideas. Then, as one moves through the early work years, our peer groups evolve through self-selection and, of necessity, we are then molded into the political beings that we become. In fact, research does indicate that contact with a group may actually lead to liberal/conservative polarization. [28]

After that, as we move through our adulthood, two other players begin to shape our political orientation. One is the *media*, which feeds us information and provides us with even more data that backs up our political views. It is quite common for us to rely on those media sources that we feel most comfortable with. This media can be television, radio or all the alternatives on the internet.

Last, but not least, are those mainstage *political actors* (politicians and political groups) that vie for our attention. By this time, our political orientation is mostly formed, and we are looking to support those who have ideas similar to our own.

Life Changing Experiences
In addition to our brain structure and political socialization, our beliefs can also be shaped by any life changing experiences, which are the shocks to our system that cause us to alter our behavior. Let us look at a few cases that illustrate this.

A classic example is Nancy Reagan, the wife of President Ronald Reagan (1981-89). Mrs. Reagan was very devoted to her husband and she supported conservative causes, such as the *Just Say No* effort to stop all drug abuse. She also played a significant role in Reagan's decisions on personnel and foreign affairs. But, when retired President Reagan developed Alzheimer's, she became a very strong advocate for stem cell research—one of those scientific research projects conservatives would normally criticize as being unnecessary government spending.

Another case of a switch from a conservative to a liberal policy, the experience of James Brady. Brady was a very staunch advocate of conservative policies within the Reagan White House until he was shot by John Hinkley Jr. That one-time traumatizing event permanently disabled Brady and turned him into a very strong advocate for gun control until his death in 2014. His wife then carried on this cause.

Ideology switching also happens on the other side of the political spectrum. Consider the example of Hillary Clinton. She was a highly reliable backer of the "get tough on crime" bill that was signed by President Bill Clinton in 1994. Then, when she was running for President in 2016, she criticized the mass incarceration that was a result of that 1994 crime bill.

What happened, in part, to cause this major shift was President Bill Clinton's relationship with Monica Lewinsky between 1995-1997. This highly-publicized scandal certainly put a major strain on the Clintons' marriage. Hillary Clinton then set off on her own political career (U.S. Senate in 2001,

Secretary of State in 2009 and as a Presidential candidate in 2016).

Or, consider the policy flip-flop of Barack Obama regarding the U.S. *Guantánamo* prison facility in Cuba, used for locking up terrorists. As a Presidential candidate, Obama argued against jailing suspected terrorists without giving them an opportunity to ask why they were being held and not giving them a chance to even prove their innocence.

After becoming President, Obama appealed a U.S. District Court ruling that gave the prisoners in Afghanistan the legal right to challenge their captivity. Obama based his case on arguments from the Department of Justice (from the Bush Administration). Then, in May 2009, President Obama introduced a dramatic expansion of his executive power. He established military tribunals (for the prisoners judged as dangerous) and noted that his Administration had a right to hold these detainees in custody, without any trial or any opportunity to present their cases.

Why did Obama make such a dramatic shift in policy? Quite simply, Barack Obama was now a President of the United States who had to face the very harsh reality of combatting the terrorist threat. This reality of becoming the President, rather than campaigning for President, was a sufficient shock to his system.

If these conservative and liberal politicians could make these major policy shifts because of significant life events, then, it is also perfectly reasonable that liberal and conservative citizens can make a switch because of some change in their lives.

Take the case of a liberal factory worker and union member who loses his job because his company is moving overseas. This individual is quite likely to switch his vote to a Presidential candidate who wants to get tough on trade and bring jobs back to America. Or, consider a case of an active conservative whose son or daughter comes out as gay; this conservative then becomes more supportive of gay rights.

External

Russia has been manipulating other causal factors (psychological, social and experiential) to reshape political behavior in the West. Russia's goal is to weaken the European countries and the United States by creating *cultures of fear* within their populations and struggles for control of their governments.

Our Disunited States of America

How does this work? This is done by targeting alienated citizens with disinformation. Those that are alienated come to believe that the *outsiders* (the immigrants and minorities) are slowly taking over their countries and that their current political leadership ignores the problem.[29]

We have seen this chaos in Europe with the Brexit fiasco that has destabilized The British Isles. Moreover, there have been similar discord efforts that have been directed against Germany, France, the Czech Republic, Greece, Austria, The Netherlands, Hungary, Sweden, Italy and Poland and the European Union. Russia has incited internal fear within these countries by disseminating anti-globalist, anti-immigrant and white nationalist dogmas through the back door.

Russia does this through a highly sophisticated methodology. One part is using computer-based websites, emails and online posts that are supposedly launched from other countries (not Russia) to supply disinformation. This creates fear as well as anger among alienated voters within the target country. Then, Russian intelligence also uses this disinformation to energize support for those anti-globalist and anti-immigrant politicians in target nations who can then challenge the status quo. The net result is political chaos, as one side of the political divide goes against the other.

Donald Jansiewicz

So, it is not unusual that the 2016 Presidential election in the United States was hacked. This propelled a candidate, Donald Trump, into an office that has resulted in high levels of controversy and the prospect of even greater controversy as we move towards the 2020 election.

Vladimir Putin is not doing this to carry out the mission of the old Soviet Union. Rather, this former Soviet KGB officer has brought all of his spy craft skills into his new role as President in order to rebuild Russia's economy (with the help of Russian oligarchs/billionaires) and restore the Russian Empire that had lasted nearly 200 years (from 1721-1917), before it was then toppled by the communist revolution.

Why is Putin going after other countries? Russia has vast territory, but it is literally surrounded by other nations that are either potential rivals or economic opportunities. Norway, Finland, Estonia, Latvia, Lithuania, Belarus, Ukraine, Georgia, Azerbaijan, Kazakhstan, Mongolia, China, Japan and Alaska (in the United States) either share a border with Russia or are near the Russian border.

More importantly, Russia lives under continuing pressure from both the European Union (EU) and the North Atlantic Treaty Organization (NATO), a carryover from the old cold war days.

The EU enabled its member nations to work together as they build their economies. In the process of doing so, Russia has been brushed aside. Russia has been frustrated in its efforts to take on an economic leadership position in Europe and has responded with such actions by cutting off energy and implementing trade embargoes against the EU countries.

The NATO countries continue to focus on Russia for good reason. From 1917 to the present, the USSR/Russia has invaded fifty-six countries. The latest examples are Russian military actions against the country of Georgia (just east of the Black Sea) and the more recent acquisition of Crimea (also by the Black Sea) from Ukraine.

Why is the Black Sea so important? Control of the Black Sea is the virtual doorway to the Mediterranean Sea through the Turkish Straits. Russian military or commercial ships will now be able to go from the Sea of Azov in Russia through the Black Sea and then on to the Mediterranean Sea.

Moscow fears the possibility of a military conflict (conventional or even nuclear wars) with NATO countries as it tries to advance its interests. And even though the cold war days are over, the West still views Moscow with great suspicion.

Russia's only way out of this NATO trap is to find ways of undermining and destabilizing member nations which might hold back Russia. If those countries undergo internal strife, then Putin will be able to achieve his goal and *Make Russia Great Again.*

In sum, we have seen how our brains and our own political socialization, as well as life events and foreign intrigue have an impact on our thinking about politics. But there is also just one more very important cause (the role of the media). So, let us now turn our attention to the media and how it also shapes the dialog between the liberals and conservatives.

Our Disunited States of America

MEDIA ECHO CHAMBERS

The media has evolved over time to become one of the most significant causes of the sharp divisions which have been taking place in our country. It does this by both facilitating and exacerbating those differences that pull us further and further apart from one another.

Let us now examine how the media is keeping us divided as a nation by providing a virtual echo chamber where both sides are being reinforced as they come into conflict with the other side.

In order to understand this echo chamber, we first need to go back just a few years and look at how the media was unleashed from government regulation. Then we will view the proliferation of media sources in our lives. Finally, we turn to how the media coverage of events and controversies turns into this echo chamber.

The Death of the Fairness Doctrine

The *Fairness Doctrine* was established in 1949, after World War II, when memories of how Adolph Hitler used the media to push ahead his agenda were still fresh. This was also the time in which television, a very new technology, was just being launched and the three television networks (ABC, NBC and CBS) were the active players. NBC and CBS got started with radio in the 1920s and ABC joined the media club in 1943. PBS began broadcasting in 1969. Then, years later in 1986, the Fox network jumped into the media game.

The *Fairness Doctrine* is not to be confused with the *Equal Time Rule* from the 1927 Radio Act. The *Equal Time Rule* applied to political candidates for office and gave them equal access to media coverage so that the elections would not be manipulated.

In the case of the *Fairness Doctrine*, the FCC (Federal Communications Commission) feared that these networks (ABC. NBC and CBS and their stations) might feed biased information to viewers about certain issues. FCC's right to take this action was based on the limited number of channel possibilities on fixed frequencies (over the electromagnetic spectrum). So, the FCC could establish the terms for issuing a license for each individual station. Given that rationale, it is not at all surprising that the FCC might create something like a *Fairness Doctrine* in order to execute its responsibilities.

Our Disunited States of America

Unlike newspapers, which can be published by anyone, television and radio stations are part of the "public domain" because of these fixed frequencies. Presenting any one-sided information from a newspaper or magazine is the right of the owner because he or she owns the business. The airwaves, however, are public property and are not owned by the radio or television stations.

Conservatives have always been quite skeptical with regard to the *Fairness Doctrine*. They saw it as just another way for "big government" to try to muzzle their free speech, violating the *First Amendment* to the Constitution. In this vein, when Congress passed a bill to turn the *Fairness Doctrine* into law, President Reagan vetoed the bill.

In 1987 the entire Federal Communications Commission repealed the *Fairness Doctrine* by a 4-0 vote. Three of those who voted had been appointed by President Reagan and the one other additional commissioner, from the Richard Nixon administration, also voted for the repeal.

Along with the repeal of the *Fairness Doctrine*, major changes were taking place in the media business in the 1990s. One substantial change was radio attempting to attract a larger audience after it lost advertisers to the internet. Secondly, radio was becoming more centralized in the hands of a smaller number of owners (Clear Channel owns over 1200 stations at this point in time). And finally, America's radio industry was then able to venture into the political arena by establishing "talk radio," in which media personalities could take one-sided positions on issues.

Talk radio quickly became one of the major advocates for conservative thought in American politics.[30] This has been particularly true since the September 11th attack in 2001. Of the 257 talk radio stations in the U.S., 236 of them are conservative. That is 91% of the talk radio stations. For every 2,570 broadcast hours from conservative talk radio there are only 254 hours of progressive or liberal talk radio.

In order for conservative talk radio to become successful, it needs an audience, and that is what they have. Those who regularly listen to talk radio stations in America are predominantly white, male, religious-in-orientation and over fifty-four.[31] This is a reliable base for these broadcasters, and it attracts advertisers who want to reach this same audience.

24-Hour Media

Media of all types are now operating nearly twenty-four hours each day. Broadcast news and cable news are there constantly, as is radio. In

Our Disunited States of America

addition to these sources, we have the internet, plus communication with each other by cell phone, email and social media.

We have been transformed into a society where we both send and receive messages throughout the day and night. This information flow never stops. None of us really needs to wait for the evening news to find out what is going on. All we need to do is turn on one of our electronic devices (radio, television, computer or cell phone) and we become engulfed in today's political drama.

Simply evaluate your own media habits. Just how much time do you spend on your phone, sending/receiving texts, working on your computer, listening to the radio or watching television? Then add up these hours and calculate the percentage of your waking hours that is spent connected to media.

This is a tremendous opportunity for liberal and conservative policy advocates. All they need to do is continue injecting new information through media in order to keep stimulating their bases.

Now that there is no expectation that media is to be fair and balanced, the diatribe between the conservatives and liberals just grows and grows. There is never a break. The old concept of a news cycle is no longer relevant. The news can come at any time of the day, and this news will be both reported and commented on continuously.

Echo Chambers

The liberal and conservative tribes both live in virtual echo chambers that keep bouncing information all around, over and over again. It begins with some issue finding its way to various media outlets. Then, these media outlets send information about this issue to the liberal and conservative base voters. These base voters then interact with each other through social media and their messages find their way back to the media. Next, these messages get picked up by other media operations for further distribution to the base voters. The base voters then get enraged and this flows back as another issue and it begins all over again. It happens over and over.

These conservative and liberal voters get driven further and further apart as time goes by. This will continue unless the two sides figure out some way to put aside their differences and see value from the opposition. But that is not likely to happen. So, the drama continues.

Our Disunited States of America

MANIPULATING OUTCOMES

The final factor which has led to this heightened diatribe between liberals and conservatives is how each side deliberately manipulates the political process in order to achieve their respective goals and, in doing so, increases the level of conflict.

Let us go over a number of strategies that increase the tension between these two tribes. Each side in this nasty struggle feels quite violated when the other side uses one of these strategies against them. However, these same people feel comfortable and justified to use one or more of the same techniques when they want to achieve *their own goals*.

Spreading False Information
One very well-established method of manipulation in politics is the strategy of spreading false information or instilling myths as well as unsupported impressions about the other side. The source person or organization doing the manipulating feels quite justified in painting a picture that will be damaging to the opposition.

You see and hear this every day. Liberals do this when claiming that conservatives are both dishonest and uncaring. Then, conservatives do this by claiming liberals waste valuable resources, hold back economic progress as well as support abnormal and inappropriate behavior.

Both of these sides do this through the media and the rumor mill. Each side carefully searches through the political landscape to pick up some tiny piece of evidence that backs up their claims.

Then, the information is spread from the source to others who pass it on to other people. Disinformation is much like the common cold or flu that is contagious and infects more and more people as it expands.

One of the dangers in using this approach is for either side to go through the agony and embarrassment of being accused of lying and being unreliable. The normal responses of those making the false claims is a complete denial or ignoring the charges.

The greatest danger in spreading false information about the other side is how it ultimately benefits Russia. Both liberals and conservatives have been used to achieve the goals of Moscow.

The anti-war movement during the 1960s was carefully manipulated by Soviet intelligence to disrupt American politics. [32] Today's Russian intelligence is now feeding propaganda to the conservative groups to further destabilize American politics and thus weaken our political system. [33] Liberals and conservatives have helped Moscow to achieve its goals. Russia is now manipulating both sides to promote our political paralysis.

Gerrymandering

Gerrymandering is a manipulation technique in which state legislators from the dominant political party pass legislation that draws the legislative district lines in such a way as to favor their political party. This approach to manipulation has been part of the political fabric in the United States for many years.

It began over two hundred years ago, when Elbridge Gerry was the Governor of Massachusetts. Governor Gerry signed a bill that stacked the deck for Congressional representation by redrawing Congressional district lines to favor just one party (his own). These districts ended up looking like a salamander (therefore the term, *gerrymander*).

The strategy of gerrymandering has been used over and over again over time. There are multiple examples throughout the United States in national, state and even local legislative offices.

According to the *Baltimore Sun*, Maryland has one of the very most gerrymandered Congressional districts in the country. This Third Congressional District stretches into several counties (four to be exact) as well as parts of Baltimore city.

The following map gives you a picture of what this worst case looks like. You can see how it stretches all over the place to capture the loyal voters that are needed.

Our Disunited States of America

There are several other examples of this gerrymandering from both the conservative and liberal states. How do such things happen? Maybe the very best way to explain these gerrymandering techniques is by creating a hypothetical state so we can see exactly how it is done.

Let us call our hypothetical state *North Rectangle*. You can see from the following *Before* and *After* charts that there are three Congressional districts. Each of these Congressional districts has blocks of voters that do regularly vote for either the Circle ● political party or the Plus + political party. These charts show you these three Congressional districts and the ● and + voters, both before and after gerrymandering.

In the **Before** gerrymandering chart, the Circle ● party has a majority (● 21 to + 9) on the left side. And, the Circle ● party also has a majority in the middle or central district (● 20 to + 10). Finally, the Circle ● party has the majority in the district on the right side (● 19 to + 11). The Circle ● party has control of all three of these districts in the Before chart. Overall, the Circle ● party has a total of 60 statewide blocks of voters and the Plus + party has only 30 blocks of voters.

Now, let us look at what happens when the Plus + party suddenly gets control of both houses of the state legislature, after unanticipated election results. Then, the Plus + party cleverly redraws the Congressional district map. Just look at the **After** map and you will see that the State of North Rectangle still has three districts; but they are arranged differently. One district at the top/left, one in the middle and one at the bottom/right.

You will also see that the middle district now is completely controlled by the Plus + party (● 0 to + 30). While the Circle ● party still has control of both the top/left (● 30 to + 0) and bottom/right (● 30 to + 0) Congressional districts.

Instead of losing to the Circle ● party in all three of Congressional districts, as it had before, the Plus + party has picked up one additional Plus +

party seat in Congress. This was cleverly done, even though the Plus + party has a minority of voters statewide.

Legislation and Executive Orders

Both liberals and conservatives can also achieve their goals through legislative and/or executive actions. Members of Congress can persuade their colleagues to pass a bill, or others can request the President to issue an Executive order.

In the legislative arena, there are many examples of this strategy. On the liberal side, there has been the legislative effort to restore the Obama era's *Net Neutrality Rule*. When it was established, it required that the Federal Communications Commission (FCC) make sure that each of the Internet providers would treat all the web traffic equally and not select what is most available online. Another example would be the legislation that is designed to keep immigrant families together instead of being split up by our national government.

On the conservative side, there was legislation that prohibited colleges and universities from obstructing the *First Amendment* freedoms. Such legislation would allow religious colleges to bar all same-sex relationships or same-sex student groups. This legislation would also block college administrators from preventing controversial speakers from presenting their ideas on campus.

Two recent executive orders are also very good examples of using an executive order to achieve ideological goals. One such case would be President Obama's order to close down the Guantanamo detention center in Cuba because inmates were being held without trial alongside allegations of torture. This particular executive order was not funded by the Republican-dominated Congress.

And, yet another case would be the executive order by President Trump, on his very first day in office, to stop federal funds going to any international groups that perform or provide information about abortions. This was a clear "thank you" message to his political base.

Electoral College Roulette
Winning the Presidency is another strategy which liberals and the conservatives use to achieve their goals. It is not just about advancing a strong candidate that can walk away with a majority of popular votes (all of the individual votes tallied up into a grand total). Rather, it is all about the efforts to win the majority in the Electoral College, which

aggregates the popular vote winners in individual states.

The magic number in Presidential elections is 270. Each state has a number of electoral votes that is equal to the seats it has in the House of Representatives plus its two Senators. Also, the District of Columbia gets three electoral votes. Of the 538 total electoral votes, the winning ticket must get a majority of 270 electoral votes. That is not an easy task.

Here are the electoral votes in the closest elections in about the last 50 years:

Year	Winner	Votes	Loser	Votes
1976	Carter	297	Ford	240
2000	Bush	271	Gore	266
2004	Bush	286	Kerry	251

Jimmy Carter won the 1976 race against Gerald Ford by only 57 electoral votes. George W. Bush won the 2000 election by just 5 votes against Al Gore. Then, Bush won again 2004 election against John Kerry by 35 votes.

There are other elections in American history when the Presidential contests were nearly as close. So, we have a clear pattern that the Presidential election is a high stakes political game that requires winning the popular votes in certain strategic states, in order to come in over the top.

The following chart[33] displays electoral votes that are practically guaranteed for the very most conservative and very most liberal states. The liberals have 142 of the "guaranteed" electoral votes and conservatives have just 55. Neither side is in a position to win. Conservatives need to add 215 electoral votes and liberals need to add 128.

Most Conservative		Most Liberal	
Wyoming	3	Vermont	3
N Dakota	3	Massachusetts	11
Mississippi	6	Connecticut	7
Oklahoma	7	New York	29
Alabama	9	Washington	12
Arkansas	6	Maine	4
Idaho	4	California	55
Louisiana	8	Oregon	7
Montana	3	Maryland	10
Utah	6	Hawaii	4
	55		142

Now, look at the next chart of remaining states and see if you can come up with the necessary number of votes for each side. That is, the conservatives need another 215 electoral votes and

Our Disunited States of America

the liberals need another 128 votes. Try your political/math skills.

21 + Votes	16-20 Votes	11-15 Votes	6-10 Votes	1-5 Votes
FL 29	GA 16	AZ 11	AL 9	AK 3
TX 38	IL 20	IN 11	AK 6	DE 3
	MI 16	NJ 14	CO 9	DC 3
	OH 18	NC 15	IA 6	NE 5
	PA 20	VA 13	KS 6	NH 4
			KY 8	NM 5
			MN 10	RI 4
			MO 10	SD 3
			NV 6	WV 5
			SC 9	WY 3
			WI 10	

Judicial Involvement

The judicial branch is able to also advance both conservative and liberal causes. This happens when a case is brought before a lower federal and state court and gets appealed all the way up to the Supreme Court. Then, the Supreme Court, the highest court in the United States, is able to make decisions, which can have a very dramatic impact on the debate between liberals and conservatives.

One of the most notable examples of this is the Supreme Court Case of *Brown vs. The Board of Education* (Topeka, Kansas), which advanced the liberals' effort to integrate public education. After this, conservatives began advocating for such things as home schools, charter schools and less funding for public schools.

Another case, this time conservative, was *District of Columbia vs. Heller,* which was decided in 2008. In this case, the Supreme Court decided that the 2nd Amendment protects an individual's right to possess a firearm. The Court ruled that a citizen has a right to own a firearm, and such ownership does not need to be connected with service in a militia.

Following this court decision, liberals responded in a variety of ways, including legal actions and demonstrations. In fact, the liberal response has escalated after several more cases of mass shootings took place in a variety of settings.

However, there have been only a few very strong responses from the government. The Florida legislature did pass some restrictions on gun owners. The National Rifle Association is standing its ground and it has a very long history of resisting restrictions on guns. The Supreme Court's ruling in the *Columbia vs. Heller* case is the law of the land.

Our Disunited States of America

MY WAY OR THE HIGHWAY

Let us now see what could happen if either of these tribes gets its way. First, we will look at what is likely to happen if conservatives have control of all three branches of government. Then, we will look at what might take place if the liberals control the Presidency, Congress and the judicial system. In either case, the tribes would have to control the whole national government for many years (maybe 20-30) in order to accomplish their goals.

In both cases, I take a "what if" approach. I will do this by describing the ideal types of policies that each side promises. In either situation, the tribe that loses would have to accept what has taken place, adjust their expectations, or just "hit the road" and go to some promised land.

So, crank up your imagination and start envisioning what could happen in a couple of decades if conservatives or the liberals have solid control of the American national government.

Donald Jansiewicz

If Conservatives Rule

At long last, Americans came to their senses and finally put dedicated conservative leaders in solid control of both houses of Congress as well as a vast majority of state governments (even in such liberal places as Massachusetts, Vermont and California). Moreover, our country has now had conservative Presidents for the last twenty-four straight years and the judicial system is now filled with responsible judges at all levels of the federal judiciary. It has certainly taken some time and effort, but America has finally gotten back to the values that have made our country a model for the rest of the world.

The liberals stopped whining and have finally given up after losing several elections over the years. People are now reading about the old "liberal establishment" days in their history books. They are finding that the liberals tried risky experiments to solve problems and that the liberals' promised results were not, and never could be, achieved.

There is no more of the silly talk about "climate change" or "global warming." The discredited scientists have just given up and only talk to each other. People are recognizing that temperatures go up and down and that sometimes the weather is unpredictable. There is a very clear recognition among most people that we humans are not in a position to make some type of divine statement about the fate of the world.

In the new America, the economy has blossomed and it just keeps getting even better. The United States has never before seen such a very prolonged growth rate. The unemployment numbers are down and productivity is rising to record levels. Also, the stock market keeps going up to record highs as the economy keeps growing and growing. America has never experienced such a blossoming of our economy.

There have been major cutbacks in the federal government's spending. Social Security has been replaced by a program called *Invest in Your Future*, in which all of the contributions, earnings and payments from individual retirement savings plans will <u>never</u> be taxed. Government regulations have nearly been eliminated, plus there is a no-nonsense type of tax policy in which everyone is paying the very same low percentage rate and there is no need for income tax write-offs, except for charitable contributions and business expenses. These tax changes have completely energized the economy.

Businesses, whether large or small pay only small corporate tax rates and have been extremely successful. Those who are wealthy are spending their money at record levels. Even those who are lower on the economic ladder have also seen their incomes steadily rise over the years. Also, the number of people who are unemployed and are looking for work has dropped to a record low.

The federal government's deficit has been all but eliminated. Our federal government officials, in Congress and the White House, have reduced it with revenue from millions of taxpayers who make far more money than ever before. Since the government does not have to support any of the unnecessary programs, the federal government is now paying off the national debt. We have never seen anything like this before.

Since its transformation into a truly conservative United States, there is once again a greater respect for the Constitution and those basic principles that the Founding Fathers believed in. Today, the three different branches of our national government, although separate, are now team players working for the common good and not just focusing on the tiresome complaints of the outliers.

This new team approach to government has been accomplished, in large part, by assuring that each of our elections are decided by the voters who are now properly registered and not by those "fake" voters who cast ballots in multiple locations. This new integrity for our elections process has been guaranteed by the state and national legislation which has stopped all voter fraud.

This program to stop voter fraud was accomplished by requiring individuals to register each year and to verify their identification and residence by providing supporting documents (birth certificate, driver's license, a tax record, an employment history, social security number and a credit report). In addition, state government authorities have done background checks every year to authenticate the identity of applicants who have registered to vote and look for any criminal records that might disqualify them.

Most importantly, there is now a deep respect for our Bill of Rights. The First Amendment's "freedom of speech" clause is being strengthened through judicial decisions which allow people to express heartfelt ideas that once would have been falsely labeled as "hate speech."

These citizens were restricted in the past by liberal politicians and interest groups. Now, our ordinary citizens are hearing devoted people speak out about those who have tried to undermine our nation. Since the old fake media has continued to wither away, the responsible media has now amplified the messages of those who are fighting for what is right and proper.

We are also in a much safer country and the crime problem is almost history. DNA records are now being kept (from when a child is born, when one applies for a driver's license and after any prior felony/misdemeanor) in order to identify those who have committed the crimes. Criminals are also being caught planning their schemes with the very new electronic information-gathering equipment (both cameras and audio recorders) that are used before the bad actors get a chance to engage in their disgusting criminal activities.

These criminals now know that they will be spending plenty of time in prison. In order to make good on this promise to lock up these criminals, even more prisons are being built in every state through creative public-private partnerships.

In addition, gun violence has been brought almost to a halt. Our teachers and other people who have regular contact with the general public are now trained to use their weapons and they routinely have their loaded guns with them. Moreover, the potential shooters have not only been quickly stopped before they can cause damage, but we are identifying potential shooters and getting them evaluated and sent to mental hospitals.

Our Disunited States of America

We have also reached that point in our country's history where the highest standards of morality are defining us. *The Family First Act* has raised the importance of moral standards by providing parent training for those who might have children as well as families that need guidance. State and local governments also have family support staff who are identifying those individuals who are troubled and may be holding back their family's progress. These "troubled individuals" are now placed into counseling to change their behavior patterns, which otherwise might undermine family values.

America's population is rising because the birth rate for traditional families is now much greater than that of the illegal immigrants and any other outsiders. These very new "made-in-America babies" are now being welcomed by devout citizens and by those very courageous "right-to-life" organizations which have worked for years to stop those who try to murder the helpless unborn.

Since federal legislation has been passed to outlaw any type of distribution of information about abortion, as well as any physician training in abortion procedures, state efforts to halt abortions have been strengthened.

Donald Jansiewicz

In addition to supporting families, state and local governments are identifying individuals who are inclined towards deviant or inappropriate sexual behavior. These individuals are found early and now receive counseling to help them develop a gender identity that will enable them to establish successful and appropriate relationships during their lives.

Because of national, state and local cooperation the traditional model of public education has been altered. Home schools and new types of charter schools have now replaced the outdated K-12 model.

Students are now given a general evaluation of reading, writing and mathematics at ages five, ten and fifteen. Then, based on their abilities, they are placed in a local charter school or home schools which can best meet the educational needs of each student. Students are also placed in contact with other students with whom they feel comfortable.

These students are now guided to those educational outcomes which are based on their natural abilities as well as their willingness to work hard. These charter schools and home schools cooperate with local religious institutions to make sure that these students are also achieving high

Our Disunited States of America

moral standards, in addition to the traditional academic standards.

Many of these things have been achieved by just concentrating on building ourselves up as a nation and not taking in as many immigrants. We have now limited our immigration to those from western European countries, Australia and Canada.

The wall separating the United States from Mexico has doubled in size (height and length) and a deep barrier has been placed under the wall to stop illegals from trying to build tunnels under the wall. Moreover, Coast Guard ships are patrolling all along the U.S. coastlines to prevent illegal entrance from the oceans and the Gulf of Mexico. Also, our army troops are now being stationed along the border with Canada to prevent illegal immigrants and drugs, from sneaking across the Canadian border in order to enter the United States.

After the United States withdrew from the North Atlantic Treaty Organization (NATO), we built more comfortable relationships with Russia. Russia has totally abandoned its communist past and is a thriving capitalist country. Very soon, the Russians may be able to immigrate to the United States and become U.S. citizens.

Donald Jansiewicz

    The United States and Russia have entered into a new *League of Friendship* in order to build more peaceful relationships. New and bold pro-Russian politicians have come into power in Belarus, Poland, Lithuania and Latvia and these countries also want to join this new *League of Friendship* and have more cooperation with the Russians.

    America has now finally achieved its goal of being the greatest country in the world. We now have the largest military on the planet and we conduct our military training throughout the world in order to respond quickly, in case of any new international problems. We also have severed all trading relationships with those countries that have refused to cooperate with the United States, or we impose tariffs on all of their imports. These tariffs provide additional federal government revenue that is used to support our domestic manufacturers.

    After the U.S. threatened to pull out of the United Nations, the UN has now agreed to America's demands. All of the members of the UN Security Council who are chosen are first deemed acceptable by the United States.

    Moreover, the United Nations is now funded by new taxes on all goods that are traded between countries, rather than the contributions made by the member countries. The UN is now able to meet many of its past goals as well as new goals, such as providing aid to countries that are trying to build up their economy. This enables these countries to now purchase the products (new cars, televisions and cell phones) and the services (internet and movies) from our American companies.

Because of America's new leadership, we now live in a world that is so much safer and better. We owe all of this to the dedicated and very hard-working conservative leaders who kept their promises, on both the domestic and international front.

It is now a much better and more peaceful world.

If Liberals Rule

America has finally achieved the ultimate position of being the most desirable country in the world, under the leadership of liberals at the national and state government levels. It has taken years for this to happen.

For far too long, Americans have longed to achieve what Scandinavian countries have accomplished. We now have a government that respects all people and helps them attain both a productive and a satisfying life. A generation, which was born in this century, has finally transformed our county's old political landscape into a new government that works for all people.

In the past years, conservatives made many of the big decisions. These conservatives were mostly older people, born in the last century, who have moved on to join their Maker. Certainly, our new generation of leaders will get older over time, but they have gained so much wisdom by watching the past generation of conservatives make such a complete mess of things.

Today, liberals are making the decisions. We have control of both houses of the Congress and have won the Presidency for the last twenty years. In addition, liberals gradually took over the positions in the federal court system that were controlled by conservatives for far too long.

After many years, we have now achieved a real full-employment economy for the past sixteen years. Everyone who is able to work is now employed. Even those who have been unable to work because of a disability are placed in a situation, either at their residence or in a local center, where they are able to engage in productive activity.

Our Disunited States of America

Today's Americans can remember what it used to be like. People were out on the streets and on the sidewalks just begging for money. They were sleeping in alleys. They needed help, but they were not getting it from a government that only looked the other way.

Now that the old politicians are gone, we have established the national policy for a "real-world" minimum wage. The amounts are adjusted for each state based on the cost-of-living in that state for the year. This new minimum wage enables workers to afford the things that they need to live a decent life. Low income employees may also get a government subsidy in order to help them with their basic expenses, if they live in very high cost communities.

In addition, the workday has been cut from eight hours a day to six hours per day. This change has not only allowed workers to have more time for the things that they want to do with their life, but it has also resulted in more people being employed to meet the needs of employers.

The old eight-hour day was established around the time of the Civil War and was in use for over one hundred and fifty years. It was certainly time for an enormous change. Our modern technology is able to free these employees from those very outmoded and obsolete work schedules.

Mass transit has increased dramatically through assistance from the national government. A very significant number of workers are able to get to their work locations through rapid rail and bus transportation. It is now normal for individuals to travel from one location to another by public transportation, rather than by automobile.

Consequently, the air pollution problem has now been finally brought under control. Outmoded, needlessly expensive and polluting automobiles have been replaced by a transportation system that meets 21st century needs. Cars still exist, but they are used for public safety needs and to help those who are unable to use public transportation.

Moreover, every individual, from birth through old age, has government-approved life and disability insurance as well as the new MedAmerica national health plan. With MedAmerica, there is no such thing as co-pays, deductibles or other such nonsense. If one needs to see a doctor, all that's necessary is to make an appointment.

The national government, in cooperation with all fifty states, has established an educational system for all students from Kindergarten through graduate school. These students are now able to pursue their educations at no cost as long as they keep making academic progress and complying with institutional regulations. The idea of debt from a college or university education is a thing of the past.

In addition, the national government is providing aid to local school systems to provide important afterschool programs. In these programs, the students work with each other on community service projects as well as additional activities that are beneficial for both the students and the larger community.

The national government is accomplishing many goals on the domestic front to improve the quality of life and the environment. This is paid from three sources. First, there is the 7% National Transaction Assessment (NTA) which is included in every purchase of goods and services. Secondly, there is a 5% income tax for those in the bottom 5%, a 10% income tax for most taxpayers and the new 75% income tax, with no write offs (except charity), for those in the upper 25% income bracket. Finally, there is a 10% tax on all the corporate earnings of any American company or of any foreign company that sells its products or services from abroad to any commercial organizations or consumers in the United States.

The national debt has been brought under control through four strategies. First, the federal government has now stopped all borrowing. Secondly, the federal budget has dramatically increased the amount allocated to pay off the debt. Third, the government is fully funding those programs that are deemed beneficial to the quality of life. And finally, the federal government has now significantly reduced military spending by cutting expenditures for those established military services (Army, Navy and Air Force) and eliminating those duplicative or overlapping military operations (Marines, National Guard and Coast Guard).

Private companies will still be able to pursue their economic goals, but must comply with all the government regulations for working conditions as well as the overall impact on the community and the environment. Companies that are in violation of these regulations are fined, and any further violations will result in the loss of their national corporate license and/or mandatory replacement of those who made the decisions to violate the regulations.

In addition to building a responsible economy, the new liberal era has also nurtured respect for those who had been marginalized in the past. Discrimination is no longer tolerated. Those ethnic, racial, sexual and gender-variations (LGBTQ) that have been discriminated against in the past are now put on a level playing field. Those that discriminate against them are identified and given fairness counseling. And finally, those who do engage in violent actions against minority group members now face very serious criminal charges.

The United States is also a safer nation. In part, the full-employment economy has reduced the crime rate dramatically. Individuals who are now employed have no reason to engage in criminal activity. And those who do engage in such activity are deemed to be "troubled individuals" and receive counseling or assignment to some institution to deal with their emotional difficulties. Prisons are now disappearing as counseling-based institutions are growing in importance.

After it was decided not to abolish the *Second Amendment*, Congress passed the *National Firearms Safety Act*, which remains compliant with the *Second Amendment*. The act restricts gun possession to only those who are serving in state militias.

In order to supply guns to the militias, the national government has taken possession of all guns that were held privately and turned them over to state militias. Former gun owners have been compensated for their firearms and they can serve in militias. Their guns are now stored in the militia facilities.

Militia members can use the guns while on duty in their monthly training sessions and must return them to the militia's local storage facilities. These actions have created a backup for the United States Army and nearly eliminated gun violence while remaining <u>consistent</u> with the *Second Amendment* militia requirement.

Political discourse has also changed in the United States. Our broadcast media must adhere to the *Fairness Doctrine* that had been discarded in the past. Networks and stations that promote only a single point of view have lost their ability to broadcast. Similarly, the internet is regulated to prevent the dissemination of blatantly false and hateful ideas.

Moreover, those individuals who seek to present false and hateful speech are facing lawsuits from those who have been injured by those comments, as well as facing major criminal charges. And, if found guilty of such a criminal charge, the offender will be sentenced to major community service projects, the length to be determined by a judge.

As society keeps evolving, reproductive choice is no longer an issue to be debated because birth control is both a right and a responsibility. A woman will no longer have to give birth to an unwanted child and there is also government support for both birth control and birth control training.

America has now transitioned into a country which is once again welcoming immigrants. The major goal is to energize our economy by bringing in the best and brightest talent from overseas, as well as being a country that takes immigrants from areas of the world that are troubled.

Moreover, the United States has discarded the idea that we have to be the major political power in the world. Instead, the U.S. has now increased its involvement with other nations in regional international coalitions (the North Atlantic Treaty Organization as well as the Trans Pacific Partnership) and the United Nations.

In addition, the United States is carefully building much stronger relations with its old adversary, Russia. This is being done through joint funding of necessary economic activities (like roads and railways, from Russia to western Europe) in order to help Russia interact more positively with these countries.

The United States will do its full share in being a part of these established international organizations, like the UN. We will provide funds and military forces when necessary. Also, the United States is now taking a major role in the environmental policies for reducing pollution, which causes climate change. We are also joining with the other nations to bring a halt to drug trafficking as well as human trafficking.

There still are some conservatives. They are old and they only get together with each other. What they talk about is what things were like in "good old days" before America changed.

INTERNAL REALIGNMENT

There are some alternatives to the *My Way or the Highway* solutions. Our political system could be legally restructured by using various approaches that could enable each side to potentially find some ways of addressing its needs, as well as reducing the level of conflict. We'll now examine each of these ways of internally realigning our political system.

States' Rights/Interstate Compacts

Two very different state-centered approaches could be used if we want to get away from those ideological struggles that have plagued our nation. Let's take a look at each of these options.

The first one of these alternatives is for each of the fifty states to base their efforts on the *Tenth Amendment* of the Constitution. This very important amendment reads as follows: *The powers not delegated to the United States by the Constitution, nor prohibited by it to the States, are reserved to the States respectively, or to the people.*

Donald Jansiewicz

By using this states' rights approach, each state can establish public policies (either liberal or conservative) that are acceptable to the active voters in that state, as long as it does not infringe on any of those rights of all citizens that are guaranteed by the Constitution. This, in fact, is already being done by states that have prevented abortions as well as those states that have regulations on gun ownership.

Those who are dissatisfied by the public policies in their current state of residence could move to another state, one that is much more compatible with their views. In this way, we Americans would be reshuffled and end up in the states in which they feel most comfortable.

The second available alternative is for the states to enter into Interstate Compacts. The very first Article of the Constitution states that *No State shall, without the Consent of Congress... enter into any Agreement or Compact with another State*. Basically, this means state governments can cooperate with each other to achieve common goals, just as long as Congress approves. State governments already have Interstate Compacts in such areas as the *Driver's License Compact*, through which states can exchange data on the drivers.

Our Disunited States of America

Likeminded states could have Interstate Compacts on a range of other issues. This approach could be used by conservative or liberal states as long as they gain approval from Congress. Imagine if conservative states wanted to establish an Interstate Compact for *Home School Support* that provided needed resources for the home schools in those states. Or imagine, another Interstate Compact that provided a *Medical Care and Pharmacy Network* for the patients in those liberal states that are part of a compact.

By using such an Interstate Compact approach, the liberals and the conservatives might be able to both avoid ideological struggles at the national level and still achieve their goals, as long as they have the approval of Congress. This Congressional approval could be achieved by having each side support the other side's compacts in an exchange for support on the compacts that they want to establish.

Unicameral Legislature
The process of passing legislation could be greatly simplified by amending the Constitution and specifying that there would only be one chamber in Congress. If done, the Senate would probably disappear. This would prevent struggles between the House and Senate.

The new House would have the very same number of members, reflecting the state's population (the District of Columbia could be counted in either Maryland or in Virginia). This new House of Representatives could also avoid the problem of gerrymandering if the Congressional district lines were drawn by a computer program that created districts that were compact, contiguous and of equal size.

Presidential Election by Congress
Another way to reduce the level of our ideological tension is to have the President be chosen by the Congress, rather than the general election. Basically, this would be similar to the British Model where the Prime Minister is selected by a majority in Parliament. The President could still be limited to two terms.

The advantage of using the British model is to create a situation where the President and Congress would be more connected and work more closely together. The President's policies are more likely to reflect the general will of the people if the President is chosen by the elected legislature.

Fixed Judicial Terms
Still another way of insulating our country against the ideological stalemates is to change the

way in which federal judges (for the District, Circuit and Supreme Courts) are chosen.

The President could nominate each candidate, and the candidate would be voted on by the Senate. However, these judicial appointments could be for fixed terms, and these vacancies would be scheduled in a way that neither ideological tribe would be able to install judges who would hold power for lifetime appointments.

Taken all together, the fixed judicial term approach along with the Presidential elections by Congress plus the one-house legislative branch and much greater reliance on state governments can help moderate the political discord we are experiencing.

Donald Jansiewicz

MODERATING FACTORS

In our contentious climate, there are some factors that can moderate the struggle and give us more time to work out solutions that are acceptable to both sides. This chapter presents five different *candles* that might provide us with enough *light* to get out of the present *darkness*. We will now take a look at each of them.

Population Shifts

A major factor that can change the level of divisive conflicts between conservatives and liberals is population redistribution. Individuals and families are, in fact, moving from their states or communities to a new location.

One part of this population shift is the movement from the Northern, Eastern and Midwestern states into the Southern and Western states. This population shift has been happening in recent years and will certainly be reflected in the next (2020) census. [34]

It will also surely have an impact on some of these states' seats in Congress, both in terms of the number of states that are impacted as well as the House and Senate members' political orientation. There can be some dramatic changes (from liberal to conservative or from conservative to liberal) in the outlook and voting patterns of House and Senate members.

The following 2016 chart[35] shows both the fastest growing states as well as the fastest shrinking states over a 10-year period.

Fastest Growing		Fastest Shrinking	
Rank	State	Rank	State
1	Utah	1	W. Virginia
2	Nevada	2	Illinois
3	Idaho	3	Vermont
4	Florida	4	Connecticut
5	Washington	5	Wyoming
6	Oregon	6	Pennsylvania
7	Colorado	7	Mississippi
8	Arizona	8	New York

You can see that nearly all of these fastest shrinking states are in the eastern and midwestern states. However, Mississippi (a Southern state) has been in decline for many years and the sharp drop in Wyoming (a western state) has taken place after nearly three decades of growth. The recent decline in Wyoming is due to rapid changes in the oil and coal industries.

The fastest growing states are in the South and in the West. Florida is the single Southern state that has been experiencing rapid growth for several years, mostly from retirees and winter homeowners. There are also many more western states in the rapid growth category.

In this overall regional population shifting, some companies have moved from their old home states to these new states, where there are more opportunities (tax breaks). Some employees have followed their companies and other workers are now deliberately moving to the growth states, where there are better prospects.

The other part of this population shifting is the movement away from the poor rural areas (within a state) to either the mostly suburban or exurban commuter towns, small metro communities and to some large urban areas. With few prospects left on the farm, the children of farmers and some farmers themselves are now building new skills and reinventing themselves in a new environment.

In any case, these mobile populations are bringing their political views with them, but they are all entering into new arenas. Because of this reshuffling process, new friendships are being formed, different perspectives are now being intermingled and individuals' views might be slowly modified.

A Greater Role for Women

Females outnumber males in this country. In 2018, 51.6% of the U.S. population was female while 49.4% of the population was made up by males (even though slightly more males are born than females). The reason that women outnumber males is because men die sooner. Males' earlier deaths are because males generally take more risks, work dangerous jobs, experience more heart disease, avoid their doctors and also have fewer social connections.[36]

Women are becoming more involved in American politics, and this may be one of the most effective ways of moderating the ideological differences in current American politics. There are three basic reasons why this pathway to moderation by female political activity could be happening.

First, women are more inclined towards moderation. You will recall the earlier chapter on *Underlying Causes*, in which a section on *Internal Cause* examined the human brain's *Right Amygdala*. As you remember, that part of the brain processes fear and becomes enlarged, in the case of political conservatives.

Data also shows that the Right Amygdala is also larger for males and is smaller for females[37]. Males lean towards conservatism, in part, because of this enlargement of the Right Amygdala. Because women don't have this enlargement, they are not so programmed towards such conservative responses.

Males are more likely to fall into the category of being fearful of those things that are different, and males often lean towards a "fright and fight" response. Women, by contrast, with their much smaller Right Amygdala are less fearful. As a result, women are more inclined to have more moderate views on issues and be more accepting of differences.

Women also have a larger *Anterior Cingulate Gyrus,* or information gathering center, which they use when choosing their sexual partners. Some also refer to it as the woman's "worry wart center," which makes them much more empathetic to others.[38]

Secondly, women are much more social and are more likely to associate with others who have different points of view. In contrast, men are less social and are more likely to keep to themselves and hold on to their political views. When these males come into contact with those who have opposing views, they are either more inclined to avoid talking to the other side or they just move into the confrontation mode.

Finally, women are playing a much greater role in American politics. This is occurring for two very important reasons that reflect the major transformation that is taking place in our country.

First, women are more likely to vote than males. This is because women have much more of a sense of civic duty.[39] In addition to having longer life spans, the increased likelihood of voting increases the total number of female voters in elections.

Voting by women has been exceeding the voting by males since 1964. Just look at the turnout in the last seven Presidential elections to see the percent of women and men who reported voting. Note that the *spread of percentages voting* (difference in female/male voting) has been trending upwards for women in those elections.[40]

	% Voting in Presidential Elections						
	1992	1996	2000	2004	2008	2012	2016
Women	66.3	59.6	60.7	65.4	65.6	63.7	63.3
Men	64.6	57.1	58.0	62.1	61.5	59.8	59.3
Spread	1.7	2.5	2.7	3.3	4.1	3.9	4.0

Projecting this into the future, it is increasingly likely that women (who have more voters and are more likely to vote) will be the deciding force in our elections.

Secondly, women are also running and winning elected offices at the national, state and local levels. This has been slowly increasing over the years—though there are still more males in office. But it is only a matter of time before things change.

Here are the percentages (after the 2018 midterm elections) of women[41] holding positions in the House of Representatives, the Senate, the state legislatures and the thousands of local government leadership positions as of 2018. It is now a little over one in five offices or slightly more than 20% for women. I suspect that it will be 50% or more in about twenty years.

Gender Distribution in American Politics		
Elected Offices	**% Male**	**% Female**
U.S. House	80.00	20.00
U.S. Senate	77.0	23.00
State Legislatures	74.6	25.40
Mayors 30,000+ Cities	78.20	21.80

Our Disunited States of America

We have had nearly a century since the ratification of the *Nineteenth Amendment* which gave women the right to vote. America is moving more slowly than many other developed countries regarding gender equality. This is for the most part due to our cultural evolution, which subtly says that a woman's place is at home raising the children.

But times are changing and women are now moving into the driver's seat.[42] *Women's Liberation*, *The Women's Movement* and the current *MeToo* movement have inspired women to become more involved. Moreover, women have been pushing ahead in both their academic as well as their career achievements. A woman has even run for the office of President and won the majority of the popular vote in the 2016 election.

Generational Differences

The political debates may also become much less contentious after the next generations take on the challenge of governing. They will certainly be playing a greater role in both the voting booths and in elected offices.

At this stage of our nation's history, America has six different generations that are relevant for our analysis and they span a time period of over a hundred years. The first of these generations got started in 1916, in the middle of the

First World War. And, the last of these generations was born from 2000 through the present.

In the one hundred years that these generations have been around, this country has experienced several wars, multiple economic setbacks and a number of major social changes. It has been a stressful time for our nation.

Let us now take a look at each of these different generations and their impact on our political system. Here is a list of each of these six different generations:

- The Greatest Generation
- The Silent Generation
- The Baby Boomers
- Gen X
- Gen Y (the Millennials)
- Gen Z

The following chart compares these six generations in terms of birth year, current size and percentage of the total population.[43]

Current Generations in American Politics

Generation	Birth Years	Size (millions)	Percent
Greatest	1916-28	3.79	1.20
Silent	1929-46	28.32	8.90
Boomers	1947-65	75.52	23.50
Gen X	1966-81	65.72	20.36
Gen Y	1982-99	79.41	24.70
Gen Z	2000-16	73.61	20.30

The Greatest Generation is now in the process of disappearing because of their age. Those that currently hold power in this country (the Silent Generation and the Baby Boomers) were born around the middle of the nineteenth century, from the 1940s through the 1950s-60s. Those in the Silent Generation grew up in post-Great Depression America and have quietly worked to achieve their goals. Post-War Baby Boomers are more self-confident and feel special.

Neither the Silent Generation nor the Baby Boomers will be around in the next few decades. After that, a new political parade will begin with Generation X, followed by the Millennials

(Generation Y) and Generation Z (those born after 1999).

According to Pew Research, Gen X, the forgotten generation, is much more inclined towards more moderate views[44]. They are 21% liberal, 23% conservative and 66% fall in-between the ideological purists.

Millennials do have divisions within their political views and some are more engaged than others. Forty-four percent of these Millennials describe themselves as being Independents. They think that neither the Democrats nor the Republican party are doing a good job of representing them. According to an NBC poll, over 70% of Millennials believe that America needs a third party that would do a better job of representing the real long-term needs of the American people.

The policy agenda that the Millennials advocate is some new kind or type of governmental activism to solve problems. Even though they seem to be more grounded in liberalism, they are trying the climb the ladder and are now seeking economic stability. They seem to be hunting for a blend of liberal and conservative policy ideas.[45]

Generation Z is also a rather mixed picture and does not fit into either the liberal or conservative mold. They tend to be rather conservative on the economic issues and are quite risk averse (they watched their elders go through the Great Recession). However, they are concerned about global warming and environmental issues. Moreover, Gen Z is more liberal on issues such as marijuana legalization, gender equality, transgender rights and racism. They don't seem to have any idea of what is meant by the "American Dream." The Gen Z numbers will soon surpass Millennials.

Gen Z is also the most diverse of any previous generation.[46] Gen Z members that were born after 2007 (what some call Z+) are approximately 49.6% percent Caucasian, 26% Hispanic, 13.8% African-American, 5.2% Asian and 4.7% Mixed Race and .8% Native American. Their agenda will reflect their diversity.

So, it looks like we may be drifting towards a less tense future, with more opportunities to find some common ground. Generations X, Y and Z have lived in an America which faced new social, economic and foreign challenges and they have seen the two tribes just point fingers at each other, make promises and spend years explaining away that they were misunderstood and not really given a chance. In any case, the old crowd (the Greatest Generation, the Silent Generation and the Baby Boom) are now in the process of leaving the stage.

Donald Jansiewicz

Revitalizing Rural/Small Town America
Those living in rural and small-town America live on 97% of the total amount of land in the country, but make up only about 18% of our country's total population. That is down from 40% back in 1900.[47]

Aside from an uptick in 2010, this rural and small-town population is still generally declining. The young have been leaving. There are fewer births and there is also increased mortality.

Rural and small-town areas face major economic challenges. Employment opportunities are currently quite limited. Moreover, wages and salaries are lagging behind other areas and household income is much lower than in metropolitan areas.

These rural/small town Americans are feeling quite distant from what has been going on in American society. They are 87% white and non-Hispanic. They believe that their values (just being friendly, sharing, looking out for their neighbors) are different when compared to values in the rest of the country. Consequently, they have viewed themselves as being the "outsiders."[48]

They have felt ignored and resent politicians that seem only interested in the cities and the immigrants. Rural residents believe that politicians only think about the rural areas when they need to build a new prison or to find a place for a new casino.

This is perhaps the biggest challenge in moderating the political divide in the country because rural and small-town America is at the core of the conservative base. Yet changes are slowly being made to upgrade the quality of life for rural Americans and transform it into a force for political moderation.

This is a work in progress and is certainly a very big challenge. The side benefit of changes would be to reduce rural and small-town America's isolation from the rest of the country. Any moderation of these differences that does occur would increase their feeling of being connected and interacting with the metropolitan areas. This upgrading can be based on several current and possible actions.

A critical step in this transformation to moderation is the gradual replacement of current family farmers and small-town businesses with young entrepreneurs.[49] As the family farmers "meet their Maker" and the kids sell-off their inheritance, these energetic newcomers arrive either to merge the multiple farms, or to align them into providers of more specialized boutique products (cheese, organic foods and other items) rather than just trying to sell the milk, eggs and crops to the mass market. Meanwhile, these business creators are establishing chains of small-town enterprises to meet local needs. Now the locals are able to drive shorter distances to get what they need.

Many of these new farmers and the new small-town business creators did not grow up on these farms or in these small towns. They bring in a whole new set of experiences and values.

Probably the most critical step is a new effort to increase rural access to communications technology.[50] This is now being done by (1) increasing the number of rural cell phone towers, (2) expanding the availability and affordability of satellites for television reception as well as (3) increasing access to the internet.

These connections do not use the antiquated land lines, and these technological improvements allow rural Americans to experience what urban/suburban people are experiencing. It could also reduce the rural sentiments that they do not count or are being ignored.

In fact, as rural America is brought up to speed with the technology, television networks will understand that these rural/small town Americans are an important part of their audience. These networks could cover more stories about rural areas. One example would be the big challenges that farmers face with agricultural production and its effect on prices. Another would be the severe drug abuse that has been occurring in rural and small-town America (one of my nephews died from a drug overdose in the small town I grew up in).

These technological tools can link rural Americans to the rest of the country and keep them from being isolated in our rapidly changing world. This will then provide more opportunities for rural Americans to interact with others, present their ideas, hear the other side and even find common ground.

Another way of helping rural small-town America is to put more resources into improving its infrastructure.[51] This can be done by paving old dirt roads, increasing water supply and electrical availability as well as trash removal/recycling (which is 2-3 times more expensive than in urban areas). These changes would create common experiences with other Americans.

In addition, there needs to be a major effort to bring them up-to-date in other areas. These areas need help with new or updated housing as older housing continues to deteriorate. There is also the need to restore funding cuts for education in many of these states, so that the rural and small-town students will be more likely to apply to, and be admitted into, higher education institutions.

Medical care availability is also currently limited, and there is a shortage of primary care physicians and nurse practitioners, as well as transportation. Rural hospitals are not a possibility. However, new rural and small-town clinics can be an effective intermediate step, especially for those situations which are serious, but not of an emergency nature.

Public safety is also another area for improvement. Crime is now increasing in rural small-town areas,[52] most likely because of limited economic opportunities and drug abuse. The small town that I grew up in has been struggling with an increase in all types of crime in recent years, and is now making slow progress in the area of public safety. Cities have been doing a more effective job with controlling crime through increased and more effective policing.

Family businesses in small towns and rural areas also need to be supported through new tax breaks as well as new transportation improvements. Those who are living in remote rural areas now have to drive great distances in order to get what they need.

Even small-town churches, which are so important in these rural areas, also need to see positive changes—in both transportation and communication—as new opportunities to possibly expand the number of their worshippers, or to connect with them in other ways.

In addition, the workforce needs to be prepared for those businesses that might want to relocate in these areas because of the economic opportunities (lower real estate prices) or in the development of tourist attractions.[51] Such changes would make rural areas less isolated and make the lives of these Americans more similar to those in urban areas.

If successful, these actions would enable the rural populations to be more stable and even to grow. The young people would not be so inclined to leave the farm and head to the urban areas. They would be able to stay much closer to their families as they begin their new lives.

Moderation Advocates

There are two major organizations (*No Labels* and *Better Angels*) that are working 24/7 to help this country moderate the self-destructive ideological insanity that we have been fed on for too long. Let us now look at each of these organizations and how they play a role to move us towards a political system that works to benefit all citizens.

No Labels (www.nolabels.org) was first launched in 2010 and is based in Washington D.C. It seeks new ways of getting us beyond the political fist fighting between the two political tribes. It advocates for new problem-solving approaches that can work for all of us.

No Labels functions as somewhat of a top-down type organization. Insiders (from both parties) who are sick and tired of the stalemate sit down with each other and develop ideas that can make meaningful changes. They energize their grass roots activists to place pressure on Congressional representatives to transform our current dysfunctional political system.

This organization has dedicated individuals who organize in their communities. They share the *No Labels* message with their community to support problem solvers, get-out-the-vote and take the lead on efforts to write letters or emails to their members of Congress and the media.

Our Disunited States of America

One of the very most important initiatives of *No Labels* is the *Speaker Project*, which is an effort to revise the role of Speaker of the House, so that the Speaker is not a roadblock to progress. Also, *No Labels* has helped create the *House Problem Solving Caucus*, which is a bipartisan group (there are twenty-four members from each party), that seeks real progress with the major issues such as the budget, the infrastructure, immigration, gun safety and healthcare.

In addition, *No Labels* distributes booklets on <u>Break the Gridlock</u>, <u>The Speaker Project</u>, the <u>No Labels Policy Playbook</u>, <u>Make America Work</u>, <u>No Labels: A Shared Vision for a Stronger America</u> and <u>Just the Facts</u>.

Better Angels (www.better-angels.org) is inspired by Abraham Lincoln's inauguration speech when he urged all Americans to get beyond the struggles that were pulling our country apart at that time. *Better Angels*, based in New York City, takes a much more bottom-up approach to addressing the problem of political dysfunction. It does so by nurturing moderation at the ground level. *Better Angels* seeks to reshape the overall discussion of our public policy issues throughout the country and moderate decisions at the top.

Donald Jansiewicz

The organization was launched in 2016 to help bring unity to our divided country. It does this by bringing conservatives and liberals together, finding new ways to talk to each and then create a more unified direction for our country. *Better Angels* creates alliances at the local level, where the Red and Blue participants work with each other to find some common ground.

Their workshops can be best thought of as a type of "marriage counseling" for our political system, in order to help mend the troubled relationship between the liberals and conservatives. Workshops are headed by an equal number of Red and Blue Organizers who try to depolarize the political dialogue.

Two Moderators (one Red and one Blue) that are provided by *Better Angels* run the meetings. During the workshops, these Red and Blue participants meet separately and discuss stereotypes about their side. Then, each group meets in a "fishbowl" session to discuss issues and they are observed by the other side. Finally, each side is able to ask questions of those on the other side. During these sessions, there is an emphasis on treating the other participants with respect.

In addition to the workshops, *Better Angels* also sponsors debates at the community level. These debates are highly structured and chaired by an individual that is trained by *Better Angels* in order to ensure that things are both consistent and even-handed. The goal is for everyone to walk away with an appreciation of the other side.

Better Angels offers training for those who manage the debates and workshops, as well as recruits and provides support for the Red and Blue Organizers for their activities.

In addition to these activities, the *Better Angels* website offers a large variety of information to get people thinking. There is material on bridging the partisan divide, *Better Angel's* mission, their media and the latest news.

Taken together, these two advocacy organizations, *No Labels* and *Better Angels*, are each offering our country meaningful approaches for substituting our national process of political self-destruction with new and fresh approaches.

Both the *No Labels* and *Better Angels* organizations need to be encouraged and supported. If they succeed, we all come out as the winners.

Donald Jansiewicz

FINAL THOUGHTS

Dear Granddaughters,

I am writing to you today to help you get ready for some major challenges that you will be facing in the future. You will not only have the challenges of making new friends, building your skills, finding a job and eventually starting your own families.

Probably one of your most difficult challenges will be your "unpaid" job of being a citizen in a country that is being pulled apart by people who think that they know it all and refuse to sit down to work out differences with others.

You didn't cause any of these problems. In fact, my parents, my generation and another generation called the Baby Boom are the ones who allowed this mess to get out of hand. We did it by permitting some people to push their own ideas down everyone's throats. These pushy people thought that they had all the answers and expected others to just follow them.

The struggle that is taking place for our nation is surprisingly similar to some things that you might already deal with on a daily basis. One of them, which you have probably seen, is what some call cliques. *The cliques are made up of kids that interact with each other on almost a daily basis.*

One of the things that happens in these cliques is that some people "bad mouth" those who are not in the clique. They feel very comfortable saying unflattering things about those who are not in their own group.

Those who are not in any clique are seen as the "outsiders" and they have to live their lives without the support of such a group of very close friends. Sometimes that outsider image makes them feel very sad and lonely. They feel rejected. That is a cruel thing to do to another person.

Then, things get worse when it comes to the bullies. These bullies seem to take great pleasure in humiliating or intimidating others. The bully makes false and threatening statements to the victim. I hope that this has not happened to you. Being on the receiving end of bully-behavior is not at all pleasant. One never feels good after being bullied.

Unfortunately, our whole country is having a real problem with cliques and bullies. Two large cliques have formed over time—one called the conservatives and the other called the liberals. Each of these cliques competes with each other in order to get more votes and then gain control of the government at all levels. They make harsh statements about those in the other clique and they even tell lies about people that they don't include in their clique.

In fact, some of those who are in these cliques are what we can truly call bullies. That is, they try to make the other people feel bad, and that actually makes them feel good. These are really mean people.

In not too many years, you will be eighteen years old, and then you will have a vote and be able to help make the choices for who runs our country. When that happens, beware of the cliques and bullies that try to get what they want by engaging in bad behavior.

There are some things that you can do as a voting citizen to keep these cliques and bullies from running the country.

First, you can do what your teacher probably told you about those who are behaving badly. Just report them to others that you know and even to those in government, as well as the media (the newspapers, radio, television, the internet and Facebook) to stop this very bad behavior.

Secondly, you can declare to those who are bullies or those in the know-it-all cliques that you will not put up with their behavior. If they ask for your support, just tell them to "go fly a kite" or to find something else to do with their lives.

Our Disunited States of America

Finally, let the world know that you will cast your vote for those who are interested in really helping, not just rule-making. Tell them that we citizens deserve much more than a government that is made up of just another bunch of cliques and bullies.

I know that you will make things better. I have seen that you are going to be very good and responsible citizens. Neither of you will allow yourself to be pushed around by the political cliques and bullies. From the very beginning of your life, I have watched you grow up and I have seen that you try to make this world a much better place. Certainly, you have seen people exclude other people and you have seen the bullies. But both of you are not and never will be that kind of person.

Love,

Grampy

Donald Jansiewicz

APPENDIX: AMICABLE DIVORCE

The current war of words between the liberals and conservatives may not be able to be resolved. States' rights and the Interstate Compact alternatives as well as changes to the legislative, executive and judicial branches may just be ignored, and fighting between the two tribes could keep escalating.

If things get bad enough, there is one more option. Put simply, the maps could be redrawn in such a way that the liberal states could become part of Canada.

The following map gives you a "before" picture. This map shows you North America (minus Mexico). You can see the United States mainland, the Canadian mainland and the location of Alaska, which is part of the U.S.

Our Disunited States of America

In this Appendix, we will look at how the Canadian option could take place and what a new or revised United States and Canada might look like, as well as the important consequences for both nations.

The Canadian Option

Let's start with how this might happen. Imagine a very contentious election in which the Republican party wins the Presidency, with a very conservative candidate. The Republicans also hold on to the U.S. Senate.

However, the liberal Democrats pick up just enough House of Representative seats, mostly from states on the east and west coasts, and become the majority party in the House. Then, things become deadlocked and neither side is able to achieve its objectives.

After several rounds of nastiness, the President's foreign policy advisors then engage in high-level secret discussions with the Canadian government about having the liberal states become part of Canada. The President wants to get rid of these liberal sources of the political struggles and create a much better situation for the country. The President's overall goal is to have both the conservatives and the liberals living in political systems that would work for them.

In the formal talks with the Canadian government that followed, the Canadian Prime Minister favored such a rearrangement, but the U.S. President insisted that Canada must give up something.

The Canadians proposed to have Canada give up the economically valuable Yukon and Northwest Territories —that are next to Alaska— for some of the American states. These two areas have some of the very highest economic growth numbers in Canada. Yukon has an extensive mining industry, potential natural gas and oil exploration as well as many tourists. The Northwest Territory has a very strong mining industry and also produces natural gas and oil. The U.S. President then agrees to this compromise.

Then, in order to get this new agreement between the United States and Canada to actually take place through the US-Canadian treaty a new Constitutional Amendment is introduced in the U.S. Congress to alter boundaries of the two governments by exchanging certain states for the two Canadian territories.

The Amendment passed both houses of Congress, with the required two-thirds majorities, because both the liberal and conservative states just want to get rid of the other side.

Then, this new Amendment gets ratified by three-quarters of the states (that also wanted to end the liberal-conservative debate). Over thirty-eight states, both liberal and conservative, agreed to this. The actual exchange took place on January 1, in the agreed upon year.

The following map shows you exactly what Canada would look like after the agreement with the United States:

Donald Jansiewicz

On the upper left part of this new map, the Yukon as well as the Northwest Territory, are gone and are now part of the United States. The lower left part of this map also shows the Hawaiian Islands, which were also removed from the former United States and are now part of Canada.

The map also shows the location of the former west coast states of Washington, Oregon and California which have now become part of the new Canada. In addition, the map shows that Canada runs across the Continent as well as the areas that extend up into the Arctic.

Our Disunited States of America

The map also shows how this new Canada drops down the Atlantic East Coast all the way to the former U.S. State of Maryland, as well as the District of Columbia. You can see a missing squarish area on the East Coast side. That is the border next to Pennsylvania, which has remained in the United States.

The new Canada still has its remaining provinces; but it now includes two new Provinces—that are some of the largest provinces within the new Canada. One is the *Atlantica Province*, which stretches along the Atlantic Ocean from the old State of Maine down to the old State of Maryland along with old the District of Columbia. The other new *Pacifica Province* stretches along the Pacific Coast from the old State of Washington to the old State of California, as well as the old U.S. State of Hawaii.

The following chart shows the former American States that make up of the two new Canadian Provinces:

Donald Jansiewicz

The Pacifica Province	The Atlantica Province
Washington	Maine
Oregon	New Hampshire
California	Vermont
Hawaii	New York
	Massachusetts
	Rhode Island
	Connecticut
	New Jersey
	Delaware
	Maryland
	District of Columbia

    Through these changes, Canada has gained some of the very most productive and wealthiest parts of the U.S. economy, helping bolster economic growth in the new Canada. Metropolitan areas within the Atlantica Province and the Pacifica Province would also help to energize the Canadian economy. Their added wealth more than compensated for the loss of income from Yukon

Our Disunited States of America

and the Northwest Territory that were given up in the trade with the United States.

The following chart identifies each of these former States as well as their gross domestic product per capita ranking[53] when they were part of the United States. You can now see how much wealth Canada would gain in this geographical trade with the United States. These are some of the wealthiest parts of the U.S.

GDP Per Capita 2018 (chained 2009 US dollars)			
Rank/Identity	Amount	Identity/Rank	Amount
1 DC	160,472	12 Maryland	55,404
2 Mass	65,545	18 N. Hamp	51,794
3 New York	64,579	20 Hawaii	51,277
4 Conn	64,511	22 Oregon	50,582
6 Delaware	63,664	25 R Island	47,339
9 California	58,619	34 Vermont	43,946
10. N. Jersey	57,084	44 Maine	38,921
11. Wash.	56,831		

Only Vermont and Maine were less economically developed than the other former states. Also note the very high gross domestic product per capita ranking for DC (due to the federal budget). That is because DC was the capitol of the old United States national government and is most likely to be the capitol of the Atlantica Province.

With the addition of the new Provinces, Canada received two extra benefits. One benefit is a reduction in its overall costs and the other is an increase in its income.

Some costs were shifted to the new U.S. in this exchange. Those former states that now make up the new Provinces of Pacifica and Atlantica had been providing more revenue to the old U.S. government than they were getting in the form of grants and "pork barrel spending."

More of the old U.S. government's largess was directed toward those more dependent states—which still remain in the U.S. Now the new United States no longer has the more affluent states to offset that support to more dependent states; the affluence benefits Canada instead.

The following chart shows the top states that were the most dependent[54] in the former United States, prior to the breakup. Basically, these former states costs for social programs, like Medicaid, had been picked up by taxpayers in those former liberal states for decades. The populations of the conservative states received a much higher return on the federal income taxes that they paid for each year. These "bottom ten" conservative state governments had the extra benefit of gaining a higher share of their revenue from the national government.

Most Heavily Subsidized States	
1. New Mexico	6. South Carolina
2. Kentucky	7. Arizona
3. Mississippi	8. Alaska
4. Alabama	9. Montana
5. West Virginia	10. Louisiana

On the revenue side, the new income generated by those in both the Atlantica and Pacifica provinces, was able to bring the long-term Canadian problem of public debt under control. The additional tax revenue enabled the new Canadian government to pay down its public debt at a much faster rate.

Moreover, the American liberals have found a new home in their move north. Their policy preferences are now fully supported within the new Canada. These liberals no longer have to struggle with conservatives on economic, social, Constitutional or international matters.

The New United States
Given the new agreement with Canada, the political makeup of the new United States would look quite different than what we are used to. The west coast and much of the east coast would be sliced away from the central as well as southern parts of the country. Basically, this new United States would be made up of the "heartland" states and the northern states (Yukon and Northwest) that were acquired from Canada.

The following two maps illustrate what this New United States looks like (minus those jurisdictions that had become part of Canada, as well as the new areas added from Canada).

Our Disunited States of America

The top map shows the State of Alaska as well as the Yukon and Northwest Territory that were acquired from Canada. In fact, the top map is almost as large as the lower map. It may be large, but it is not highly populated.

The lower map shows the remaining territory in the USA. The west coast states were removed as well as those east coast states from Maine down to Maryland and DC. Those which remain in the new U.S. are the north Central, Southwestern, Midwestern and Southern states.

Donald Jansiewicz

The following chart shows which states remain in the United States as well as the **Northwest Territory** and **Yukon** that are being added as the two new states. In total, the new United States now has 37 states.

The New United States				
Alabama	Illinois	Minnesota	N. Carolina	Tennessee
Alaska	Indiana	Mississippi	North Dakota	Texas
Arizona	Iowa	Missouri	Ohio	Utah
Arkansas	Kansas	Montana	Oklahoma	Virginia
Colorado	Kentucky	Nebraska	Pennsylvania	W. Virginia
Florida	Louisiana	**Northwest**	S. Carolina	Wisconsin
Georgia	Michigan	N. Mexico	South Dakota	Wyoming
Idaho				**Yukon**

The new United States is a larger country and gains the economic potential from the new Northwest and Yukon states. In fact, these new states are economic engines that can raise the GNP for the new United States.

That helps offset the smaller contributions of those less productive states (Mississippi, Idaho, West Virginia, Arkansas, South Carolina, Alabama, Arizona, Kentucky, Montana, Florida, New Mexico, Tennessee, Missouri, Michigan, Nevada, Louisiana,

Our Disunited States of America

North Carolina, Oklahoma and Utah). These were all states that had lower GDP rankings, from 30 to 50 or the bottom 20%, in the "old" United States.

Access to the ocean is also much more limited. There is no longer any easy access to the Pacific Ocean, aside from Alaska, without having to make some type of arrangement with the Pacifica Province in the new Canada.

Moreover, there is also less access to the Atlantic Ocean. Access is now only from Virginia, North Carolina, South Carolina, Georgia and Florida. There is also access to the Gulf of Mexico from Florida, Alabama, Mississippi and Texas.

Products sent from the lower half of the new United States would have to be shipped via the ocean, or flown, in order to reach the states of Alaska, Yukon and Northwest. A treaty with the new Canada might allow these American products to move to those northern states through the road or rail system that runs through the new Canada.

Also, the new United States faces a major budget problem that is larger than Canada's. Its revenue has been sharply reduced and its ability to support any expensive programs is extremely challenged. Taxes would need to be raised in those states that have had the smallest amount of resources. Moreover, and it is a big issue, the very large United States national debt has become even more difficult to pay off.

There is a good chance that some individuals in the new United States might make the decision to just sell their American assets and move to the new Canada. Moreover, it just might also happen that some or all of the Great Lakes States (Minnesota, Wisconsin, Michigan and Illinois) as well as Virginia might also to want to leave new America and join the new Canada.

On the positive side, the new America conservatives have gotten what they wanted. Their new America is able to really unleash free market capitalism, adhere to those fundamental principles in the United States Constitution, maintain traditional social values and have a get-tough policy in international affairs.

Acknowledgements

I would like to thank Mary Jansiewicz, my wife, for her help with editing the text as well as the graphic images. Also, I would also like to thank my daughter, Eva, for her neuropsychologist's validation of the material on the brain. I wanted to be very sure that what I was writing about the human brain was really supported by respected research and not just someone's impressions.

Finally, I would like to thank Max Neiman, Harry Stein, Judy Gach, Joel Lapin, Suzanne Rudnitziki, David Bagwell, Judy Alden, Lucie Pasquale and Peter Farrow for their suggestions.

End Notes

1. www.news.gallup.com/poll/203204
2. www.graphiq.com/stories/5037/ranking-presidents-least-most-conservative
3. www.media.journalism.org/2014/10/21/political-polarization-media-habits/
4. www.opensecrets.org/orgs/list.php
5. www.opensecrets.org/outsidespending/nonprof_summ.php?cycle=All&type=viewpt
6. www.history.com/topics/first-ladies/eleanor-roosevelt
7. www.hbr.org/2015/04/the-4-types-of-small-businesses-and-why-each-one-matters
8. www.retaildive.com/news/small-business-saturday-sales-shrink/512101
9. www.statista.com/statistics/270001/distribution-of-gross-domestic-product-gdp-across-economic-sectors-in-the-us/
10. www.cnbc.com/2017/09/25/what-the-20-largest-retailers-in-america-pay-their-employees.html
11. www.measuringworth.com/slavery.php
12. www.federalsafetynet.com/us-poverty-statistics.html
13. www.aei.org/publication/income-inequality-and-iq/
14. www.pewresearch.org/fact-tank/2017/05/03/key-findings-about-u-s-immigrants/ft_17-05-03_immigrants_countries_3/

15. www.takepart.com/article/2015/09/29/2065-most-immigrants-wont-be-coming-from-south-of-the-border/
16. www.americanimmigrationcouncil.org/topics/immigration-and-crime
17. www.pewresearch.org/fact-tank/2017/05/03 key-findings-about-u-s-immigrants/ph_16-06-02_foreign-bornbreakdown/
18. www.people-press.org/2018/03/01/the-generation-gap-in-american-politics/
19. www.disabilitycompendium.org/sites/default/files/user-uploads/2016_AnnualReport.pdf
20. www.demos.org/blog/7/7/15/unemployment-disabled-adults-80
21. www.talkpoverty.org/2014/09/19/disability-cause-consequence-poverty/
22. www.snopes.com/fact-check/politiqs www.theglobeandmail.com/life/the-hot-button/study-links-low-intelligence-
23. www.ucl.ac.uk/news/news-articles/1012/10122301
24. www.psychcentral.com/blog/liberal-conservative-brain-differences/
25. www.ncbi.nlm.nih.gov/pmc/articles/PMC3572122/
26. www.businessinsider.com/psychological-differences-between-conservatives-and-liberals-2018
27. www.ncbi.nlm.nih.gov/pmc/articles/PMC3572122/

28. D. G. Meyers and J.M Twenge, Social Psychology 13 McGraw-Hill, Edition 2019
29. Malcom Nance, The Plot to Destroy Democracy: How Putin and His Spies are Undermining America and Dismantling the West Hachette Books, 2018
30. www.americanprogress.org/issues/economy/news/ 2007/07/10/3297/talk-radio-by-the-numbers/
31. www.statista.com/statistics/699946/news-talk-radio-audience-share/
32. Stanislav Lunev, Through the Eyes of the Enemy, Regnery Publishing, 1998.
33. Malcom Nance, The Plot to Destroy Democracy: How Putin and His Spies are Undermining America and Dismantling the West Hachette Books, 2018
34. www.news.gallup.com/poll/203204/wyoming-north-dakota-mississippi-conservative.aspx
35. www.usatoday.com/story/money/economy/2018/01/15/fastest-growing-and-shrinking-states-closer-look/1019429001/
36. www.health.harvard.edu/blog/why-men-often-die-earlier-than-women-201602199137
37. www.quora.com/Why-do-males-have-larger-amygdala-than-females
38. www.sharecare.com/health/brain/womens-brains-differ-from-mens
39. www.jwi.org/articles/hear-us-vote

40. www.cawp.rutgers.edu/sites/default/files/resources/genderdiff.pdf
41. www.cawp.rutgers.edu/current-numbers
42. www.cawp.rutgers.edu/sites/default/files/resources/genderdiff.pdf
43. www.knoema.com/egyydzc/us-population-by-age-and-generation
44. www.pewresearch.org/fact-tank/2014/06/05/generation-x-americas-neglected-middle-child/
45. www.achieveagency.com/research-shows-millennials-see-activism-in-different-way-than-previous-generations/
46. www.businessinsider.com/generation-z-profile-2017-9
47. www.scholars.unh.edu/cgi/viewcontent.cgi?article=1004&context=carsey
48. www.denverpost.com/2017/06/17/poll-rural-urban-america-culture/
49. www.smallbiztrends.com/2017/01/small-town-business-ideas.html
50. www.usda.gov/media/press-releases/2018/08/01/usda-invests-97-million-rural-broadband-infrastructure-improve
51. www.usda.gov/media/press-releases/2017/12/14/usda-highlights-40-million-infrastructure-investments-rural
52. www.thecrimereport.org/2018/05/14/rural-violent-crime-rate-rises-above-u-s-average/

53. www.statista.com/statistics/248063/per-capita-us-real-gross-domestic-product-gdp-by-state/
54. www.wallethub.com/edu/states-most-least-dependent-on-the-federal-government/2700/

www.ingramcontent.com/pod-product-compliance
Lightning Source LLC
Chambersburg PA
CBHW031151020426
42333CB00013B/611